OXFORD
UNIVERSITY PRESS

Blackstone's Police Investiga
Mock Examination Paper 2(

GW01571675

Pack 1

Contents

OXFORD
UNIVERSITY PRESS

Great Clarendon Street, Oxford, OX2 6DP,
United Kingdom

Oxford University Press is a department of the University of Oxford.
It furthers the University's objective of excellence in research, scholarship,
and education by publishing worldwide. Oxford is a registered trade mark of
Oxford University Press in the UK and in certain other countries

First edition published in 2004
Ninth edition published in 2012

Impression:1

British Library Cataloguing in Publication Data

Data available

ISBN 978–0–19–966202–9

Printed in Great Britain by
Ashford Colour Press Ltd, Gosport, Hampshire

Acknowledgements

I would personally like to give thanks to Paul Connor and Jenny my daughter for assistance with proofreading this publication. I also very much appreciate the support over the years of my friend, Darryl Winn, and that of my wife, Diane, who has helped in the logistics of this product.

Dave Pinfield

Introduction to the Mock Examination

The views expressed below are those of the author, David Pinfield retired, formally a DS training development officer at the Detective Training School, Tally Ho.

The rationale for this publication is that many students embarking on the National Investigators' Examination (NIE) have not sat a formal examination of this type, albeit a small number will have had the experience of the Part I Sergeants' examination. The preparation for the NIE is daunting as it involves having to learn in excess of 500 pages of text in a 14-week time frame; this is far more intense than either the Sergeants' or Inspectors' examinations.

On the market at present there are few products to assist candidates and those that exist are designed for Part I Sergeants'. A large proportion of the material covered is not included in the NIE syllabus. There is no road traffic or general police duties, and the crime areas are reduced in comparison. Sexual offences, however, is one part of the Sergeants' syllabus that equates to potentially 25% of the NIE. These products are helpful but not designed for you. There is an excellent publication on the market—the *Blackstone's Police Investigators' Q&A 2013*—written by a colleague, Paul Connor, that contains 300 questions specifically designed for the NIE student: this is a good test of knowledge but cannot re-create the pressure of an examination. When unsure, the temptation to look at the answer is awesome and, although this publication provides an excellent revision tool, it does not test you as a potential candidate on the day of the examination. All forces have introduced a policy whereby a candidate who is unsuccessful on the second examination will be removed from the three-tier Trainee Investigator process.

My personal opinion is that you should take this mock examination between three and four weeks before the examination. You will have had time to revise (eight weeks) but still have sufficient time left to correct matters. You need to bear in mind that to pass this examination, and these statistics are based on my experience of previous candidates in my own force (seven exams), you need to complete approximately 114 hours' revision. This figure is an average, but demonstrates the amount of work and commitment needed. I would seriously suggest that you book annual leave before the examination.

The examination contains 80 questions broken down into four areas (Evidence; Property Offences; Assaults, Drugs, Firearms and Defences; and Sexual Offences), and there will be approximately 18 questions on property, 17 questions on assaults, 13 questions on sexual offences and 28 questions on evidence. These figures do fluctuate between exams but gives an indication of what to expect. You will soon realise that there are many more areas to test in evidence compared with sexual offences, so your revision plan needs to take account of this. Within the 80 questions there are 10 validation questions, which do not count towards your overall mark. These are questions that are being tested against a strict quality assurance process to ensure all questions have equal status. They are placed anywhere in the examination and they cannot be identified, so you will not be able to take less notice of them. To pass the examination you will need to answer correctly 39 out of 70 questions. However, because of these verification questions, to be sure of a pass you need to obtain a mark of 54 out of the 80 questions.

You have two hours to complete the examination at an examination centre. The examination usually takes place the first Tuesday of either March, June, September, or November, but this is subject to change. You will need to arrive at the examination centre 30 minutes before the examination starts. To date this has always been 1.30 pm for arrival at the test centre and 2.00 pm for commencement of the examination. Failure to be there at the allotted time will prevent you taking the examination.

The format and rules of the NIE are exactly the same as for the Sergeants' examination, and there are many instances of candidates who have been delayed not being allowed to enter the examination room. You will be working hard to prepare for this examination: DO NOT put yourself under pressure by running late on the day of the examination. To gain entry to the examination centre you need to hand in a pink registration form (sent to your force) and show your warrant card. Your mobile phone has to be left in a receptacle at the rear of the examination room as modern technology could allow you to photograph or send a text after the examination begins, to assist a colleague. You will not be allowed to leave in the first or last half-hour of the examination. All examination centres across the country start the examination at the same time. There is a senior invigilator who will read out all the rules relating to the examination: listen carefully to them. Examples of possible reasons why you could be removed from the examination include opening the exam paper before being told to do so or omitting to hand in your mobile phone. There will be other invigilators at the centre to assist in setting up the room and to ensure that everyone abides by the rules. If you wish to leave the room to go to the toilet you will be escorted there and back by an invigilator of the same sex.

This mock examination is designed to simulate the NIE conditions. You have 90 seconds per question. Some of the questions are much shorter than others but no question exceeds 250 words. Each question contains a story or account, known as the 'stem'. A 'lead-in' follows: this is the question. Then you will be required to select an answer from the four possible answers, marked A, B, C and D. Multiple-choice questions using roman numerals as answer options are NOT contained in this examination, for example:

A (i) and (ii)
B (ii) and (iii)
C (ii) only
D (iii) only.

You will find that on occasions the question will seem very easy and, through your revision, you will be able to identify the correct answer almost immediately. This mental effect will give you confidence for the next question. On other occasions, you will see a question and be able to narrow it down to two options. Some students will be of the belief that the two examples they have ruled out are stupid or ridiculous. This is not the case: it is knowledge that you have which has allowed you to make that decision. Question writers will give four viable options, only one of which will be the right answer. For example, see below:

Who was previously the Labour Home Secretary before the Conservative Party took power?

A Alistair Darling.
B Robbie Williams.
C Alan Johnson.
D Oliver Letwin.

I hope you all realised that the answer is 'C'. Your knowledge should have immediately removed B. Oliver Letwin is a Conservative MP, so a bit harder, making D incorrect. You are then down to the final two. They are both Labour: one previously was the Home Secretary and the other was previously the Chancellor of the Exchequer. That question was easier because of your knowledge of the subject. Now for one where many of you will have less knowledge.

Where in the human body are the Islets of Langerhans?

A The inner ear.
B The brain cortex.
C The pancreas.
D The spine.

Answer C. How many of you were correct on this one? Unless you have studied biology or suffer with diabetes you are unlikely to know. Do not waste time on this sort of question if you have no idea of the correct answer, as there will be no divine inspiration; select and move on. There will be long questions that need time for you to comprehend fully what is being asked so do not waste time on something you do not know. That is not to devalue any question, whether it is hard, easy, or in between; they all have a value of 1.42% towards your end result.

All the questions in this mock examination are written not only to test you but also to prepare you for the examination. In the actual NIE the answer sheet is smaller than the one provided here and it could be easy to make a mistake. Do not decide to miss a question with a view to returning to it later, as if under pressure you forget, all your answers could be one out. For example, if you miss out question 36 because you do not know the answer, and move on to question 37, you could easily put the answer to question 37 in the blank row for question 36 in error. I can assure you that I have had at least one student where I am convinced from their result, and knowing the hard work they have put in, that their result was an admin failure.

An optical reader reads the answer sheet: it picks up the pencil marks on your sheet. Therefore, if you have answered B and then rub it out and put D, but have not fully erased the incorrect option, it will void this as it will show two answers. So, if you wish to mark anything to remind yourself later, use the question paper NOT the answer sheet, as even pencil marks outside the marking matrix will void the question. If you do have to erase an answer, ensure you do it with care.

All the very best in this examination: luck should not be required.

Dave Pinfield

Instructions for Completion

READ THE WHOLE OF THE INSTRUCTIONS BEFORE ATTEMPTING THE MOCK EXAMINATION

If you want to get the most from this mock examination then you must treat it as if you were sitting the examination proper.

Time

You have up to two hours to complete the examination. It might not take you that long but it is best to assume that it will, so please make absolutely sure that you set aside two hours. You cannot expect to sit part of the examination for one hour, take a break for 20 minutes, return to the examination and then get an accurate picture of your performance. The examination must be completed in one two-hour sitting. If you want to, why not try and complete the examination between 14.00 hours and 16.00 hours, as this is the time period you will sit the examination proper in 2013? You should have been told by your respective police force that the pass mark is 55% in order to bring the pass mark in line with the Sergeants' and Inspectors' examinations. This means that you now need to obtain 39 correct from the 70 marked questions.

Environment

You need to be able to concentrate on the examination and you cannot do that if the television is on, the phone is ringing, etc. Find a place where you will not be disturbed for the two hours this examination will take and make sure that there are no distractions that will affect your performance.

Equipment

Ideally, you will sit at a single desk to take the examination, but I appreciate that in most cases this will not be possible. However, you will need a table and chair of some description. Trying to fill out the answer sheet on your lap whilst holding the question paper open will prove to be a difficult task to say the least.

Make sure that you can see a clock, stopwatch, or wristwatch. It would be best to have two timepieces, just in case one stops.

You will need two pencils, a pencil sharpener, and an eraser.

Pack 1

In Pack 1 you will find a blank answer sheet and the question booklet. Place both documents on the table.

When you decide to start the examination, please open the question booklet. Work through the test questions and make your choice of A, B, C or D by putting a horizontal line through the corresponding letter on the answer sheet.

Do not make any notes or doodles on the answer sheet. If you wish to make any marks, do so on the question booklet.

Only mark one answer for each question. If two or more choices are made then the question would be marked as incorrect in the examination proper.

Make sure that if you change your answer you erase the previous mark fully.

If you leave an answer blank then it would be marked incorrect in the examination proper. Try not to leave blank answers when you are unsure. Mark an answer and come back to the question if you have time at the end of the examination.

Pack 2

When you have finished the examination, open Pack 2 and begin the marking process. When you have finished marking your paper, please refer to the answer booklet for a detailed explanation of the correct answers with paragraph references to the *Blackstone's Police Investigators' Manual 2013*.

The marking process will take some time—to ensure accuracy; please do not rush this stage!

Blackstone's Police Investigators'
Mock Examination Paper 2013

Question Booklet

Time Allowed—120 minutes

1. Each of the questions is followed by four possible answers, only ONE of which is correct. Choose the ONE response that you consider to be correct. On the answer sheet mark the box that corresponds to your selection. Mark your answer clearly with a — mark. The answer sheet has spaces for your answers to all questions. If you change your mind about an answer, rub out the first mark, then mark your new answer. Mark only one answer for each question.

2. You are reminded that there is no need to read the whole examination paper before beginning to select answers to the questions posed.

3. You must ensure that BEFORE the close of the examination all of your answers to the questions have been correctly entered on the answer sheet. If you leave a question unanswered for any reason, it will not receive a mark.

4. You may make any notes you wish on the question papers.

1. TI SANDERS approaches DC COOPER and asks for advice re the taking of intimate samples from VIOLET MEARS (18 years) who has just come into custody on suspicion of murder. The victim of the murder is JANE FREEMAN (17 years). FREEMAN was killed as a result of a bite mark to her neck severing the carotid artery two days ago. Forensics has been unable to identify any DNA of the offender from the wound. TI SANDERS asks if a dental impression could be taken in these circumstances. Intelligence shows that FREEMAN and MEARS were having a consensual sexual relationship and foreign pubic hair has been found on FREEMAN's pubis region. TI SANDERS also asks if a sample of MEARS's pubic hair could be taken in these circumstances.

   In relation to the taking of intimate samples, assuming that the correct authorisation and consent of MEARS has been obtained, which is the correct advice DC COOPER should give TI SANDERS?

   A No authority is required for the dental impression as it is not an intimate sample but it would be required for the pubic hair sample from MEARS.
   B Yes in these circumstances, both samples required are intimate samples and can be taken from MEARS.
   C Only the dental impression can be taken as an intimate sample in these circumstances.
   D Neither the dental impression nor the pubic hair sample can be taken in these circumstances.

2. KINSELLA and TARRANT are walking in the local shopping centre looking for options to steal some monies. They decide that the best way is for KINSELLA to stand at the top of the escalator, and TARRANT to wait at the bottom of the escalator, which they do. When there is a large group of people on the escalator, KINSELLA pushes the person at the top and this has a domino effect and persons tumble, losing their footings. HUGHES a female at the bottom of the escalator falls to the ground from the effect of people behind her stumbling. TARRANT takes her purse which has fallen to the floor beside her. TARRANT then runs off. TARRANT runs out the shopping centre removes the cash and debit cards from the purse and discards it. As TARRANT makes his way back to KINSELLA to split the spoils, he sees a young female CARTER in a lower underground car park and because she is alone, TARRANT decides that he will sexually assault her. TARRANT pushes CARTER violently to the ground between two parked cars. CARTER's short skirt rides up exposing her knickers. As TARRANT is about to sexually assault her, he notices the bag she has dropped appears to have the takings from a store or similar. TARRANT changes his mind and just takes the bag with the cash, not sexually assaulting CARTER.

   In relation to robbery contrary to s. 8 of the Theft Act 1968 only, which of the statements below is correct?

   A KINSELLA and TARRANT are guilty of robbery in relation to HUGHES.
   B KINSELLA and TARRANT are guilty of robbery in relation to HUGHES and TARRANT for robbery of CARTER.
   C KINSELLA and TARRANT are not guilty of robbery in relation to HUGHES as no person was put in fear; however, TARRANT commits robbery against CARTER as force was used on the victim.
   D KINSELLA and TARRANT are not guilty of any robbery in both of these circumstances.

3. The law of 'Provocation' was changed on 4 October 2010 and replaced by 'Loss of Control' contrary to the Coroners and Justice Act 2009. For the charge of murder to be reduced to manslaughter the loss of control has to comply with a qualifying trigger. Section 55 of the Coroners and Justice Act 2009 details the qualifying triggers.

Which of the statements below is not a qualifying trigger under s. 55?

   A The defendant's fear of serious violence from the victim against another identified person.
   B The fact that the thing done or said constituted sexual infidelity.
   C To a thing or things done or said which constituted circumstances of an extremely grave character.
   D The defendant's fear of serious violence from the victim against the defendant.

4. KINNOCK is an adult male and he is travelling home on the local train. Sitting next to him is ROGERS, also an adult male. When they go through a tunnel, when the train is in darkness for just a few seconds, ROGERS strokes KINNOCK's thigh. KINNOCK is unaware of what has happened.

Considering only s. 3 of the Sexual Offences Act 2003, does ROGERS commit an offence?

   A Yes, but you would have to prove sexual gratification.
   B No, the touching has to be sexual, for example an intimate region of his body.
   C Yes, in these circumstances the touching would be classed sexual.
   D No, because KINNOCK was unaware of the touching and the touching was by a person of the same sex.

5. LENNON lives on a housing estate and he has been causing serious problems for RUTHERFORD, an old man who lives at the end of the street. LENNON has an order to keep away from RUTHERFORD and his property. LENNON decides that he is going to sort out RUTHERFORD. LENNON takes with him an imitation firearm and knocks on RUTHERFORD's door. When he opens the door LENNON puts the gun to RUTHERFORD's head, intending him to fear that his life is in danger and that the gun is real. RUTHERFORD believes his life in danger and passes out. Following hospital treatment RUTHERFORD makes a full recovery and is released.

In relation to s. 16 of the Firearms Act 1968, does LENNON commit the offence?

   A No, for this offence to be committed it would need to be a firearm, not an imitation.
   B Yes, he intended that RUTHERFORD would fear his life was in danger.
   C No, as RUTHERFORD made a full recovery.
   D Yes, he intended that RUTHERFORD would fear his life was in danger and that RUTHERFORD believed his life was in danger.

6. The Forgery and Counterfeiting Act 1981, s. 5 details what are 'specific instruments' for offences contained in s. 5.

   Which of the below is not a specific instrument as defined in s. 5 of the Forgery and Counterfeiting Act, 1981?

   A Inland Revenue stamps.
   B Vehicle registration documents (V5).
   C Credit cards.
   D Share certificates.

7. The Halton Shopping Centre is being targeted by a small gang of shop lifters during the Xmas rush and you wish to use the CCTV at the shopping centre for directed surveillance, to gather intelligence and identify the offenders. This is both proportionate and necessary.

   Which of the following is correct with regard to persons who can authorise under the Regulation of Investigatory Powers Act (RIPA) 2000?

   A Must be authorised by an ACC, or orally in urgent cases; if not available in urgent cases can be authorised by a Superintendent, in which case it only lasts for 72 hours.
   B Must be authorised by an ACC, or orally in urgent cases; if not available in urgent cases can be authorised by a Superintendent, in which case it only lasts for 48 hours.
   C Must be authorised by a Superintendent or above; can be orally in urgent cases or authorised by an Inspector in urgent cases. Authorisation orally by Superintendent or authorised by an Inspector only lasts for 48 hours unless renewed.
   D Must be authorised by a Superintendent or above; can be orally in urgent cases or authorised by an Inspector in urgent cases. Authorisation orally by Superintendent or authorised by an Inspector only lasts for 72 hours unless renewed.

8. DENNINGS, an adult male, is out shopping at his local shops when he sees TRENT, an adult female, walking down the street. He approaches her and says, 'Do you fancy a quick shag?' TRENT, taken aback by what he has said, increases her pace to get away. DENNINGS grabs hold of the pocket of her trousers; she pulls clear and makes her way home.

   In relation to the offence of sexual touching contrary to s. 3 of the Sexual Offences Act 2003, does DENNINGS commit the offence in these circumstances?

   A Yes, DENNINGS has committed the offence, as it includes the touching of a person's clothing.
   B No, as the touching of the clothing would need to be covering a more intimate part of the body.
   C Yes, but he would have the defence that the touching of the clothing was not for sexual gratification.
   D No, for an offence of touching it must be shown that the part of the body touched must be considered by a reasonable person to be sexual.

9. TRANTER and FIELD are both adult males and go out with the intention of seriously injuring DAVIS. They are all drug dealers and DAVIS has been stealing TRANTER's and FIELD's clients. Neither TRANTER nor FIELD actually take drugs and are solely dealers. TRANTER takes a gun with him and FIELD is aware of this fact. When TRANTER and FIELD confront DAVIS he is in the company of KYTE. They all engage in a brawl and TRANTER and FIELD are losing out to DAVIS and KYTE. TRANTER removes the gun from his jacket and shoots DAVIS who dies instantly; shocked, TRANTER drops the gun, FIELD picks up the gun and shoots KYTE who dies later in hospital. At court it is established that TRANTER suffers from severe paranoid schizophrenia and the court accept this as a recognised medical condition and his ability to exercise self-control.

Considering s. 2 of the Homicide Act 1957 which of the below statements is correct?

A TRANTER and FIELD are both guilty of murder of KYTE and DAVIS.

B TRANTER is guilty of murder of DAVIS and manslaughter of KYTE, FIELD being guilty of murder of KYTE and manslaughter of DAVIS

C TRANTER is guilty of manslaughter of DAVIS and KYTE, FIELD being guilty of murder of both DAVIS and KYTE.

D TRANTER would be guilty of manslaughter of DAVIS and FIELD guilty of murder of KYTE.

10. PC EVERETT has been a police officer for only four months; the last two weeks he has been performing operational duties. PC EVERETT has completed 10 shifts in that time on the neighbourhood team with his tutor. On the Saturday night he is off duty and has arranged to meet his family in a nearby town; they are visiting other relatives, whom he has not seen for five months since training began, as his family home is several hundred miles away. PC EVERETT takes the bus so that he can have a couple of drinks. The bus stops at some traffic lights and PC EVERETT can see a serious fight ensuing between two men in one of the alleys off the main road; nobody else is in the vicinity. PC EVERETT can see the one male beating the other with a baseball bat. PC EVERETT decides to look the other way as he knows that if he intervenes he could be hurt and he is a bit scared, and alerting the authorities would mean he would not see his family because of the time taken up with making a statement etc.

Does PC EVERETT have any liability for his actions?

A PC EVERETT has not completed his probation so therefore he is not expected to place himself on duty.

B PC EVERETT has omitted to act, but he would be able to defend his actions owing to the fact that there is no requirement in law for him to put himself at risk.

C PC EVERETT is off duty, so can make a choice as to whether to act or not and there is no responsibility whatever his decision.

D PC EVERETT is under an obligation to act as a police officer and so therefore liable.

11. DANIELS visits the Police Station at 04:00 hours and goes to the reception desk and speaks to DC CRUMP, who is the only person in the front office at that time. DANIELS says to the officer 'I have just killed my wife and chopped off her head and she is back at our house.' DC CRUMP can see hanging from DANIELS' belt a short bladed sword and there is blood dripping from it. DC CRUMP formally arrests DANIELS on suspicion of murder.

Which of the following statements is correct with regards to seizing of the short sword?

A DC CRUMP can search DANIELS under s. 32 of PACE and seize anything that may assist his escape and evidence relating to the offence committed or any similar offence.

B DANIELS cannot be searched in these circumstances at this time, only when authorised by the custody sergeant.

C DC CRUMP can search DANIELS only if the arrest has been witnessed, because the arrest took place at a police station.

D DC CRUMP can search DANIELS but only if another officer is present, for his own safety.

12. WILSON has been arrested for drug-related crimes. At the custody block the arresting officer informs the custody sergeant that there is evidence that WILSON has swallowed some drugs. WILSON's detention is authorised and the officers wish to do an X-ray or ultrasound scan on WILSON.

In order to comply with s. 55A of PACE which of the statements below is correct?

A The drug swallowed must be a class A and have been for supply or export and the authority required is that of an Inspector and no force can be used and WILSON has consented in writing.

B The drug swallowed must be a class A and have been for supply or export and the authority required is that of an Inspector and force can be used.

C The drug swallowed can be a class A, B or C and have been for supply or export and the authority required is that of an Inspector and no force can be used and WILSON has consented in writing.

D The drug swallowed can be a class A, B or C and have been for supply or export and the authority required is that of an Inspector and force can be used.

13. JULIA BOWLES is an 18-year-old female and is currently in care of the social services at Hathaway Lodge. BOWLES has learning difficulties and has to be supervised in her daily life. JANE BOWLES is JULIA's older sister and rents her own flat. JANE is passing Hathaway Lodge at 02:00 hours, having been out for some drinks, and JANE texts JULIA and asks her to go away with her to the seaside for two days. JULIA receives the text and leaves Hathaway Lodge and they both go to the seaside, staying at a friend's house and returning two days later.

Does JANE BOWLES commit an offence under s. 49 of the Children Act 1989 (acting in contravention of a protection order or police protection)?

A Yes, all the elements of the offence are present and apply to children 18 or under.

B No, as JANE has to physically remove JULIA from care, it does not include incitement to remove.

C Yes, but JANE would have the defence that she is a direct relative and took JULIA away for less than 72 hours.

D No, as this only applies to children under 18 years.

14. BATERSBY works at a credit card company and steals from his employer 10 blank credit cards, that were supposed to be disposed of by company staff, and takes them home. BATERSBY approaches RAVEN a known fraudster in his local pub. BATERSBY explains to RAVEN that he has the blank cards and asks him if he is interested in purchasing them. BATERSBY also states that he can get access to data for the credit card blanks from the credit card company where he works, if RAVEN wishes. RAVEN unsure of BATERSBY's credibility to supply the items, turns down both offers.

Considering only s. 7 of the Fraud Act 2006 (making or supplying articles for use in frauds) in relation to BATERSBY's liability, which of the statements below is correct?

A BATERSBY only commits the offence in the making to supply the credit card blanks as he has these in his possession to supply.

B Neither the credit cards nor the credit card data are articles in relation to the Fraud Act, therefore no offence is committed under s. 7.

C BATERSBY commits the offence in the making the offer to supply both the credit card blanks and the ability to obtain the data for the blank credit cards.

D BATERSBY would commit the offence only when he supplies either the cards or the data to RAVEN.

15. JULIE MULLEN is a single-parent mother and has a son, JAMES MULLEN, aged 16; his girlfriend is DIANE KINSELLA, aged 15. JULIE is aware that JAMES and DIANE are having sex, albeit she does not allow them to have sex in her house. In view of this JAMES and DIANE visit his father, ADRIAN MULLEN, at weekends and he allows them to share a bedroom knowing that they have sex. JULIE, her son JAMES and DIANE are going on holiday to Spain and when JULIE books the holiday, JAMES and DIANE persuade JULIE to allow them to share a bedroom knowing that they will have sex.

In relation to s. 14 of the Sexual Offences Act 2003 (arranging or facilitating the commission of child sex offences), do either JULIE or ADRIAN commit an offence?

A ADRIAN is guilty of facilitating and JULIE is guilty of arranging sex for another (JAMES).

B Neither is guilty of this offence as the arranging or facilitating sex for themselves or others is for persons aged 18 or over committing child offences.

C ADRIAN is guilty of the offence of facilitating but JULIE is not guilty of arranging because the sex will not take place in this country.

D ADRIAN is guilty of the offence of facilitating because the sex has taken place; however, JULIE will not be guilty until they take the holiday.

16. DAVE and SUE have been living together for the last three months with SUE's two young children from a previous relationship. DAVE does not work but makes a few quid from minor crime and also has a violent nature. DAVE returns from the pub at 11pm one evening having had a few beers. SUE has gone to bed, so he goes to the bedroom. DAVE intimates to SUE that he wants sex but SUE states that she is too tired. The two children are staying at SUE's mother's for the night. DAVE demands sex and says to SUE that if she does not comply with his wishes then he will give the children a good hiding on their return the following day. SUE does not believe that he will hit her but knows that he would carry out his threat on the children. SUE, to keep the peace, has sex with DAVE, penis to vagina.

Considering s. 75 of the Sexual Offences Act 2003 (Evidential presumptions and consent), does DAVE commit the offence of rape?

A DAVE clearly commits the offence of rape as violence was threatened and it does not have to be the victim.

B DAVE does not commit rape as the violence threatened was to the future.

C DAVE would commit rape if he carried out his threat the following day.

D DAVE does not commit rape as the threat was to another person, which did not involve sex.

17. PC FROST attends Queen Catherine's School during school hours, responding to a complaint by the principal TREVOR FLINT that two large windows have been smashed. It transpires that some pupils may have information with regards to the damage, one being PAUL HURST, aged 16 years. PC FROST decides to interview at the school premises under caution; this is with agreement of the principal FLINT, who will act as the appropriate adult. The parents have been informed and have agreed as they are too far away to attend. Unsure of the rules under these circumstances, PC FROST phones DC WATSON for advice.

Considering the facts above, which of the following is the correct advice DC WATSON should give the officer?

A In these circumstances the interview cannot be conducted as the principal cannot be the appropriate adult because the damage was against the school's property.

B The interview can be conducted as the parents cannot attend and the principal can act as an appropriate adult.

C The interview cannot be conducted as a parent or guardian must be the appropriate adult on all occasions when interviews are conducted on educational premises.

D The interview can be conducted as the parents cannot attend but the principal's nominee has to be the appropriate adult in these circumstances.

18. The Theft Act 1968, s. 24 describes what constitutes 'stolen goods' for the offence of handling.

    Which of the below statements is correct with regards to the definition under s. 24?

    A Only property that has been stolen in England and Wales constitutes stolen goods.
    B Property obtained by the offence of blackmail is not stolen goods.
    C Money withdrawn from an account dishonestly after wrongful credit has been deposited is stolen goods.
    D Property restored to the owner in certain circumstances can still be considered to be stolen goods.

19. HOLLOWAY is the security guard at a large office block in the city. He has the responsibility of turning off two of the three power switches each evening after staff have left. The third one remains on for emergency lighting and power to the lifts. This is a cost-saving initiative by the company. This operation takes place at 19:00 hours, ensuring all staff have left the premises. One evening HOLLOWAY falls asleep and wakes at 19:15, realising he has not turned off the two power switches and in a daze from just waking up and without checking all staff have left, he turns off all three power switches. Unbeknown to HOLLOWAY, MILES, an employee, is in the lift, which stops between the 10th and 11th floors. Owing to the fact that there is no power, the lift alarm does not sound. There is a safety mechanism on the lift which, if the power is cut, uses a weight system to lower the lift slowly down to the ground floor, which it does. HOLLOWAY turns the power on ten minutes later, realising he hasn't checked, and MILES is released uninjured.

    What offence(s), if any, has HOLLOWAY committed in relation to false imprisonment and/or kidnap?

    A HOLLOWAY commits no offences of either kidnap or false imprisonment as neither can be committed recklessly; both of the offences require intent.
    B HOLLOWAY commits both offences as they can both be committed recklessly. He falsely imprisoned MILES and there was a carrying away without consent.
    C HOLLOWAY does not commit false imprisonment as this cannot be committed recklessly, but does commit kidnap as there was a taking or carrying away and kidnap can be committed recklessly.
    D HOLLOWAY commits false imprisonment recklessly, but for kidnap the person carried away has to be accompanied.

20. DC FLACK works on the drug squad and has been noting the activities at 7 Longdon Road (owner not found) and land to the side of the premises which is partially fenced off and derelict (owner also not found). The derelict land is where 9 Longdon Road used to stand, but has been demolished. 7 Longdon Road and the land are being used by many persons dealing and injecting class A drugs and is a serious nuisance to residents. Police have logged many attendances to the dwelling and the land and some arrests have been made for supply and possession of class A drugs. The relevant period from the arrests may allow for a closure notice to be served on the house or land. Consultation has been held with the local council and steps to trace the owners have been made to no avail.

Which of the following is correct in complying with s. 1 of the Anti-social Behaviour Act 2003 allowing closure notices to the premises and/or the land under certain conditions?

A The arrests have brought about at least one conviction of a class A drug crime of some person found on the premises within three months (relevant period) and is authorised by a Superintendent or above but can only apply to the dwelling, not the land as the land is not premises.

B The arrests for supply or possession for a class A drug of some person found on the premises, a conviction is not necessary, within three months (relevant period) and is authorised by a Superintendent or above for both the dwelling and the land.

C The arrests for supply or possession for a class A drug of some person found on the premises, a conviction is not necessary within three months (relevant period) and is authorised by a Superintendent or above but only applies to the dwelling not the land as the land is not premises.

D The arrests have brought about at least one conviction of a class A drug crime of some person found on the premises within six months (relevant period) and is authorised by a Superintendent or above for both the dwelling and the land.

21. Early one morning when FOSTER is out walking through some woods, he sees some blackberries growing wild. He decides to pick them so he can make several pies and then freeze them for the winter months. He continues his walk and sees a rabbit running ahead of him and he shoots it. Before he gets to the kill, JOHNSON (also in the woods) having heard the gunshot, sees the dead rabbit, which JOHNSON takes unbeknown to FOSTER. FOSTER searches but cannot find the rabbit so he goes home. FOSTER makes his blackberry pies and, realising that he has no meat for dinner, decides to sell the pies to a local farmer's shop nearby so he can purchase meat for his dinner.

In relation to s. 4 of the Theft Act 1968, which of the following statements is correct with regards to what is property?

A Only the rabbit is property when JOHNSON takes it.

B The rabbit is never property as it is a wild animal, and neither are the blackberries as they were growing wild.

C The rabbit is property when JOHNSON takes it and the blackberries are property when FOSTER picks them.

D The rabbit is property when JOHNSON takes it and the blackberries are property when FOSTER sells them commercially.

22. DOBBS is a well-known drug dealer in Thornton town and also owns a night club. He is notorious in the area for his criminal behaviour, but all prosecutions have been unsuccessful. DOBBS asks READ, a local builder, to quote him for a new roof to his garage block. READ's quote is for £4,500—a realistic price for the work—and DOBBS tells READ that he will pay in cash. READ suspects that the money is from DOBBS's ill-gotten gains, but accepts the job as his business is struggling in the economic climate. READ completes the work and is paid in cash and declares the full amount of this as income on his accounts. DOBBS is arrested 18 months later and a successful prosecution brought against him for drug dealing.

Does READ commit an offence of Acquisition, Use and Possession of Criminal Property, contrary to s. 329 of the Proceeds of Crime Act 2002?

A No offence is committed as DOBBS was arrested more than 12 months after the money was paid to READ.

B Yes, READ is guilty of the offence as he suspected that the money came from criminal activity.

C No, as READ received the money as adequate consideration for the work he completed.

D Yes, because he accepted cash suspecting DOBBS's criminal activities and this assisted in its disposal.

23. Officers raid 76 The Banks, Salford following intelligence of the persons responsible for several burglaries in the area residing at the address. The suspects are arrested and taken into custody. PC HALDER is placed at the gate of the front of the property because of local media interest, just inside a taped off cordon, whilst other officers search the property. After a short while a news team with cameras set up opposite the premises outside the taped off area. STONE one of the brothers of those arrested arrives at the property and is very annoyed that his brother has been arrested. STONE approaches PC HALDER and leaning over the tape he shouts, 'You fucking pig, if these cameras weren't here, you shit, I'd beat the crap out of you!'

Which of the following statements is correct with regards to offences of assault only?

A STONE commits the offence of s. 39 common assault as he intended PC HALDER to apprehend the immediate infliction of unlawful force.

B STONE only commits the offence of attempt s. 39 common assault as there was no battery.

C STONE commits the offence of assaulting a constable in the execution of his duty even though he used only words.

D STONE does not commit an assault in these circumstances.

24. CUTHBERT is an adult male and he befriends LITTLE, a 16-year-old female at the local gym over a two-month period. CUTHBERT fancies LITTLE and after one of the gym sessions he offers to take her home in his car. A short time into the journey he pulls off the road and forces her into the back of the car. He then pushes a candle into her vagina, penetrates her anus with his fingers and then forces a banana into her mouth, all against her will.

Which of the following statements is correct in relation to s. 2 of the Sexual Offences Act 2003 (assault by penetration)?

A All three acts constitute an offence under this section.
B Pushing the candle into her vagina and penetration of her anus digitally constitute the offence.
C Penetrating her anus with his fingers is the only offence under this section, as it must be part of his body that penetrates the victim.
D Penetration of the anus and mouth constitute the offence, but for penetration of the vagina it must be with his penis.

25. KEVIN aged 18 years, DANNY aged 17 years and ALF aged 16 years have all been charged with an offence of burglary of a dwelling house. There are many similar offences for them all to be interviewed for in respect of the police investigation of a spate of burglaries in the area. An application is to be made to the court for them to be remanded in police detention so these matters can be dealt with.

Considering the powers to remand persons to police detention after charge under s. 128 of the Magistrates' Courts Act 1980, which of the below statements is correct for the maximum time they can be remanded?

A All three can be remanded into police custody for a maximum of 72 hours.
B KEVIN and DANNY can be remanded for 72 hours but ALF can only be remanded for 24 hours.
C KEVIN can be remanded for 72 hours but both DANNY and ALF can only be remanded for 24 hours.
D KEVIN and DANNY can be remanded for 72 hours but ALF can only be remanded for 48 hours.

26. CHANDLER has just committed a burglary at 14 Haynes Croft and is running from the scene. CHANDLER's description is given to passing patrols and PC WINN sees CHANDLER. CHANDLER runs up a narrow alleyway so PC WINN gets out of the police car and gives chase. PC WINN closes in on CHANDLER, and to slow down the officer giving chase, CHANDLER tosses a metal dustbin behind him into the path of the officer. PC WINN trips over the dustbin and on falling to the ground hits his head and knee on the concrete path. This factures the officer's knee and causes cuts and bruising to his head. CHANDLER makes off and is later arrested by other officers.

Considering offences contrary to the Offences Against the Person Act 1861 which of the statements below is correct?

A CHANDLER had no intention to commit grievous bodily harm so he has therefore committed an offence under s. 20.

B CHANDLER's actions were to inflict rather than cause grievous bodily harm so he has committed an offence under s. 20.

C CHANDLER has committed an offence under s. 18 as he has maliciously and with intent to resist arrest caused grievous bodily harm.

D CHANDLER's actions are only sufficient to support a charge of assault with intent to resist arrest under s. 38.

27. CLARK is a 13-year-old female and her friend is TRANTER a 12-year-old female. They are at CLARK's house whilst their mothers are out shopping and are talking about sex and boys at their school. CLARK says to TRANTER. 'Let's go to my bedroom, I'm going to get changed.' They both go to CLARK's bedroom. In the bedroom CLARK removes all her clothes and lies on the bed as TRANTER looks on. TRANTER says 'What are you doing?' CLARK says 'Touch me down there [meaning her vagina] like a boy would.' CLARK states that she doesn't want to and leaves the room. CLARK gets dressed and they go downstairs and watch television until their mothers return.

In relation to s. 8 of the Sexual Offences Act 2003 only, does CLARK commit the offence?

A Yes, s. 8 includes incitement so the offence is made out in full.

B No, as CLARK is under 16 years.

C Yes, but it would be an attempt of 'causing' as no actual touching took place.

D No, as CLARK is under 18 years.

28. SPENCER is going away for a weekend break and he tells his friend DANIELS that he can use the house whilst he is away to watch TV as there are important matches on over the weekend on Sky which he knows DANIELS doesn't have. SPENCER asks him also to feed the cat whilst he is away and keep an eye on his property as there have been burglaries in the local area. On the final day before the return of SPENCER, DANIELS whilst watching the TV notices that on the fireplace behind the clock is a sum of money. DANIELS counts it to find that there is £60 in three £20 notes; being short of cash he puts the money in his pocket. DANIELS goes to the kitchen via the hallway to make himself a coffee. When making the coffee in the kitchen he decides to look around for anything else of value. On the end shelf he sees an iPhone which he also takes and places in his pocket. Having drunk his coffee he walks back into the hallway, pauses and thinks he'd better make it look as though someone has broken in after he has left. DANIELS decides to re-enter the kitchen and break a window to make it look like burglary. DANIELS enters the kitchen and breaks the window.

Which of the below statements is correct with regards to DANIELS's criminal actions?

A DANIELS has committed two accounts of theft and one of criminal damage.

B DANIELS has committed theft when he took the money in the living room and burglary when he stole the iPhone and criminal damage to the window.

C DANIELS has committed three burglaries; one of the money and one of the iPhone and when he entered the kitchen with intent to break the window.

D DANIELS has committed two thefts and a burglary when he entered the kitchen with intent to break the window.

29. TRENT comes home from work and finds that he has a leak in his roof. He phones a local builder, NOBLE, from an advertisement, and NOBLE visits his house. NOBLE informs TRENT that he has four loose slates on the roof, which are causing the leak. The reality is that NOBLE has no idea what is wrong but fixing the slates will earn him some cash. TRENT decides to obtain another quote for the work and uses the other builder.

In relation to s. 2 of the Fraud Act 2006, which of the statements below is correct?

A There was a false representation; however, because NOBLE did not carry out the work no offence is committed.

B A false representation has been made and the fact that the work was not carried out is irrelevant.

C NOBLE did not cold-call TRENT and it would only be in these circumstances that the false representation would be an offence, if no work is carried out.

D NOBLE commits an attempt under s. 2 as he falsely represented the work required.

30. JANET WILSON (25 years) is the English teacher at the local comprehensive school and is responsible for the A level students. DAVID BANNER is a 17-year-old student in her class. WILSON fancies BANNER and requests that he stays back after class so she can go through his course work with him. When all the other students have left WILSON tells BANNER of her feelings for him and he becomes unnerved by what she says. WILSON persuades BANNER to go into the storeroom and states that if he does as she asks he will obtain a top mark for his course work towards his exam. In the storeroom WILSON removes her skirt and pants. BANNER stands there bewildered. WILSON then moves over and kisses BANNER and then she places his hand on her vagina. BANNER then runs out of the storeroom.

In relation to s. 4 of the Sexual Offences Act 2003 (causing a person to engage in sexual activity without consent), at what point does WILSON commit the offence?

A When WILSON states that she fancies BANNER and takes him into the storeroom.
B When WILSON removes her skirt and pants.
C When WILSON kisses BANNER.
D When WILSON places BANNER's hand on her vagina.

31. JOHN FAGAN is a 21-year-old male and has been quite successful in his life as a part-time footballer and singer in a rock band and has never come to the notice of the police for any crimes. Whilst at one of his concerts he meets JULIE LANGLEY and they start a relationship, having a couple of drinks one evening and going to the cinema on another occasion. LANGLEY is 15 years of age but tells FAGAN that she is 17 years, which he has no reason to doubt. Two weeks into the relationship. FAGAN asks if LANGLEY wishes to stay at his flat overnight on the Friday after one of his concerts as it will be a late finish about 3am. LANGLEY agrees and stays at his flat on the Friday night and returns to her parents on the Saturday morning.

Considering only an offence under s. 2 of the Child Abduction Act 1984 which of the below is correct with regards to FAGAN?

A Yes, he commits the offence in these circumstances as this is an offence of strict liability.
B Yes, he commits the offence but would have the defence that he believes that she had attained the age of 16 years.
C No, as FAGAN is under 24 years and has not committed a similar offence.
D No, as he is not a connected person (parent or guardian) and did not take her out of the UK.

32. JOHN DANIEL lives in a small penthouse flat in a major city; it is his own property. Whilst ironing he knocks over some coffee onto the carpet. Owing to the fact that the carpet is of a light colour all efforts to remove the stain are unsuccessful. He believes that in the circumstances it is unlikely that he would be able to claim on his insurance. So DANIEL deliberately leaves the iron on the carpet to scorch it, knowing that this will allow him to obtain full compensation from his contents insurance cover.

Does DANIEL commit an offence of criminal damage contrary to s. 1(1) of the Criminal Damage Act 1971?

A Yes, he has intentionally damaged property which includes damaging your own property.
B No, you can never be guilty of damaging your own property.
C Yes, but this only applies because it was done with intent to commit a fraud.
D No, he would not be guilty of damaging his own property in these circumstances.

33. HENSON is arrested in Edinburgh for an offence of theft at 09:00 hours. He is dealt with by 10:00 hours for that offence and intelligence checks show that DC KEAR in Dover, Kent, requires him for an offence of robbery. As a result, DC KEAR and DC BANNER drive to Edinburgh, arriving at the police station at 14:00 hours. They do not question HENSON about the offence and travel back with him towards Dover. They cross the border with England at 15:30 hours and continue to Cambridge Police Station, arriving at 18:45 hours. At Cambridge Police Station they only have refreshment and use the toilet facilities and continue their journey. They arrive at Ashford Police Station in Kent at 21:25 hours and use the toilet facilities. They then continue the journey to Dover and arrive at 22:10 hours and HENSON's detention is authorised.

In relation to HENSON, when does his relevant time commence?

A 21:25 hours, when they stop at Ashford, even though they only use the toilet facilities.
B 22:10 hours, when his detention is authorised at Dover Police Station.
C 18:45 hours, when they stop at the first police station in England, even though they only use the police station facilities.
D 15:30 hours, when they cross the border into England.

34. CALDICOT has been arrested by TI WALKER for the offence of a s. 47 assault, and following a s. 18 PACE search in relation to the assault, property was seized. The property seized was stolen mobile phones. During an interview, CALDICOT admits the assault offence; however, he denies theft of the phones. It is established that he could not have stolen the phones and therefore he is re-interviewed in respect of handling the phones. To these questions he gives no comment. He is charged with both a s. 47 assault and handling. CALDICOT has a previous conviction for theft some two years ago.

In order to prove that CALDICOT knew or believed the goods to be stolen, in relation to s. 27(3) of the Theft Act 1968 (guilty knowledge in cases of handling and theft), which of the following statements is correct?

A Evidence of his previous conviction can be given to the court to show that he knew that the goods were stolen, provided that 14 days' notice has been given to him of the intention to prove the conviction.

B Evidence of his previous conviction can be given to the court to show that he knew that the goods were stolen, provided that seven days' notice has been given to him of the intention to prove the conviction.

C Evidence of his previous conviction cannot be given as he has been charged with another offence.

D Evidence of his previous conviction cannot be given as he has been charged with another offence which is not a dishonesty offence.

35. JOHN YATES and his wife JOANNE have been having problems in their marriage and as a result police are called to their house one evening. It is apparent to the officers that JOANNE has been suffering domestic violence, therefore culminating in the arrest of JOHN. PC RAVEN, the officer dealing with the case, takes a witness statement from JOANNE and the statement highlights three incidents. Three weeks ago JOHN came home and found that JOANNE had not tidied the house to his satisfaction and he had scratched her arm. A few days later the same happened and he grabbed both her upper arms and squeezed hard causing multiple bruising; and on the night of the police attendance, dissatisfied with JOANNE's appearance— her hair being too long for his tastes—whilst she was asleep on the settee he had cut off her small ponytail.

Considering only offences contrary to s. 47 of the Offences Against the Person Act 1861, which of the following statements is correct?

A All three assaults are offences contrary to s. 47.

B The multiple bruising to the upper arms is the only offence contrary to s. 47.

C The multiple bruising to the upper arms and the cutting of the hair are both contrary to s. 47.

D Only the scratches to the arm amount to an offence contrary to s. 47.

36. NELSON goes into an expensive jewellers and requests to look at a Rolex watch displayed in the window. KATE the assistant shows NELSON the watch which is priced at £3,000. Whilst KATE is dealing with another enquiry, NELSON decides that he does not want the watch and leaves it on the shop counter and leaves the shop. JANET, another shop assistant busy with a customer, places some papers on top of the Rolex watch on the counter. When KATE returns she sees that NELSON has left the shop and believes he has stolen the watch as she cannot see it. KATE alerts HASKINS, the security guard, to what has happened and he goes after NELSON. HASKINS is a very large gentleman and catches up near to NELSON. NELSON on seeing HASKINS is scared and begins to run. After some 200 yards NELSON sees the open rear doors of a van which belongs to a theatrical company. He reaches into the van and finds an imitation firearm. He points this at HASKINS stating 'Fuck off, I've done nothing wrong'. HASKINS turns and goes back to the shop.

Considering the offence of using a firearm to resist arrest contrary to s. 17(1) of the Firearms Act 1968, has NELSON committed the offence?

A Yes, the offence is complete; he has made or attempted to make use of a firearm or imitation to resist arrest.

B No, for NELSON to commit this offence it must be a lawful arrest.

C No, it does not matter that he is not in possession of the firearm in order to resist arrest but it does not apply to imitation firearms.

D No, for this offence he must be in possession of the firearm or imitation firearm.

37. JOHN and KATE SUMMERS live with their two daughters, MICHELE who is 15 years old and FIONA who is 18 months old. JOHN works five nights a week (Monday to Friday) at a factory; MICHELE attends the local school and looks after FIONA Tuesday and Wednesday nights whilst her mother works two evenings at the local pub. KATE has no other employment. Over a period of several weeks FIONA becomes very weak and cries a lot of the time. Although they are aware, neither JOHN, KATE, nor MICHELE seeks assistance and neither do they do very much to placate FIONA. One morning FIONA is found to have died and the subsequent investigation shows that the cause of death was malnutrition, having not been given any food.

Considering only s. 5 of the Domestic Violence, Crime and Victims Act 2004 (causing or allowing the death of a child or vulnerable adult), which of the following statements is correct?

A JOHN and KATE are guilty of the offence as the crime can be committed by an act or an omission; MICHELE is not liable as she is under 16.

B Neither JOHN, KATE, nor MICHELE are liable under this legislation as the offence is only committed where violence is used against a child or vulnerable adult.

C JOHN, KATE, and MICHELE are all liable under these circumstances, as they all either directly or indirectly caused the death of FIONA.

D KATE and MICHELE would be liable as MICHELE is over 14 years old. JOHN would not be responsible under this legislation as he is not the father of FIONA.

38. CS spray is a prohibited weapon which all police officers carry, together with some officers authorised to have prohibited firearms and ammunition.

Who is responsible for the authorisation of police officers to carry these items?

A The Police Authority for the force area.
B The Chief Constable of the force area.
C The Secretary of State.
D The Home Secretary.

39. There is a motor show at the National Exhibition Centre in Birmingham. LANE goes to the motor show and while looking at the various vehicles notices the new model Ferrari. He enters the stand and views the vehicle, but is moved on by the security staff. Later that afternoon the Ferrari is roped off with a sign 'Private Keep Out'. LANE, disappointed that he did not get to see the vehicle as much as he wished and annoyed that he was moved on, decides to enter the roped off area and take the vehicle, it being near to a wide entrance so he could easily drive out of the building; he will then later dump the vehicle. LANE climbs over the rope and soon realises that the car is a show model and that the engine that can be seen through the rear glass window is in fact polystyrene. LANE then out of frustration gets a coin from his pocket and scratches the side of the front offside wing. At the front of the vehicle he sees the Ferrari badge is slightly raised, being loose, so using the coin he prises the badge from the car, he then puts it in his pocket and goes home.

In relation to the offence of burglary which of the following statements is correct?

A LANE does not commit burglary as the roped off area is not premises.
B LANE commits burglary when he climbs over the rope and enters the roped off area.
C LANE commits burglary when he scratches the front wing of the Ferrari.
D LANE commits burglary when he takes the Ferrari badge from the front of the car.

40. ROGERS is an adult male and has arranged to meet FLOWERS an adult female as they have been identified on a dating website as compatible. It is the first date and neither of them is in a current relationship. They meet at the Duke pub and ROGERS asks FLOWERS what she would like to drink and she requests a large glass of red wine. They get on well together and ROGERS believes there is chance that they can go to his flat for sex when she orders her third glass of wine. After the third glass of wine, FLOWERS admits that she is a bit drunk but the conversation between them continues. ROGERS suggests that they go back to his flat and FLOWERS agrees. At the flat ROGERS makes a drink of coffee and FLOWERS kisses him. ROGERS goes to his bedroom to tidy it up and when he returns to the living room FLOWERS has fallen asleep. ROGERS covers FLOWERS with a blanket and goes to bed.

In relation to an offence under s. 61 of the Sexual Offences Act 2003 (Administering a substance with intent), does ROGERS commit an offence?

A Yes, he supplied alcohol which is considered a substance under the Act, the fact that no sexual offence took place is irrelevant.
B No preparatory offence is committed as FLOWERS was aware of what she was drinking.
C Yes, but for the offence to be complete some sexual activity needed to take place so this would be an attempt to commit.
D No, because alcohol is not a substance for the purposes of s. 61.

41. LUMLEY, an adult male, is questioned by DC ATHERLEY with regard to two offences of burglary and he admits his part in the crimes. At court, he is sentenced to a hospital order owing to his drug habits and mental state. After four months he is released from hospital.

There is no case to appeal, so in relation to the retention periods of relevant case material, how long does DC ATHERLEY need to retain the material?

A Once LUMLEY is released, the case material can be disposed of as he served more than three months of a hospital order.

B Once LUMLEY is released, the case material can be disposed of as there is no need to retain it when a hospital order has been given.

C The material must be kept for at least 12 months after his release, if his sentence had been custodial; however, for hospital orders it only needs to be retained for six months from the date of release.

D The material must be retained for a period of at least six months from the date of the hospital order.

42. ANDREWS incites DUNN to assault PRICE; this is because PRICE has been trying to chat up ANDREWS' wife. DUNN goes to the Red Lion public house, where he knows PRICE will be. DUNN has taken with him a small wooden truncheon and sees PRICE standing at the bar. DUNN lashes out at PRICE's face, but misses him, hitting COX the landlord, who is standing nearby, breaking COX's jaw.

Is ANDREWS responsible for the assault on COX, considering the 'doctrine of transferred malice'?

A Yes, he is guilty of the assault in these circumstances, even though the doctrine of transferred malice does not apply.

B No, there can be no transferred malice for the offence of incitement in these circumstances; it would apply only if the intended victim was injured.

C Yes, even though ANDREWS has no intention of the victim being COX he would be guilty under the doctrine of transferred malice.

D No, the doctrine of transferred malice does not apply to accessories.

43. TRANTER is known to have committed several robberies during 2001 in the Sandford area; however, he has only just been apprehended in 2011. It is established from the evidence that he stole many mobile phones, which he sold for monies to FULLER. FULLER was not sure whether the phones were stolen, but did suspect that they were but was unaware of the modus operandi of the crime.

In relation to offences under s. 327 of the Proceeds of Crime Act 2002, which of the following statements is correct with regards to TRANTER's and FULLER's liability?

A TRANTER and FULLER are both guilty in these circumstances; it matters not that the thief takes part, or that FULLER only suspects the goods to be stolen, or that the offences were committed before the commencement of the 2002 Act.

B TRANTER is guilty even though he is the thief, but FULLER must know or believe the goods to be stolen and not just have a mere suspicion.

C TRANTER is not guilty of this offence as he is the thief; however, FULLER is guilty as he only needs to suspect the goods are stolen and it matters not that the offence was committed before the commencement of the 2002 Act.

D Neither TRANTER nor FULLER commit offences under this legislation as the dates of the offences are before the commencement of the 2002 Act.

44. TI RYDER has completed his suspect interviews with DANIELS and he will be charged under s. 2 of the Sexual Offences Act 2003 (assault by penetration) by the custody officer, Sergeant BENSON, in compliance with Code C para 16.1 of PACE. DANIELS has a previous conviction in 1993 for manslaughter, for which he was sentenced to 5 years' imprisonment.

To comply with s. 25 of the Criminal Justice and Public Order Act 1994, which of the statements below is correct?

A Sergeant BENSON cannot give bail in these circumstances as both offences are covered by s. 25; when persons are charged with certain offences he has to refuse bail.

B Sergeant BENSON, even though both offences are covered by s. 25, can give bail if there are exceptional circumstances.

C Sergeant BENSON can give bail in these circumstances because although both are serious offences they have to be like offences for s. 25 to apply.

D Sergeant BENSON can give bail in these circumstances as the previous conviction was before the Act was implemented, so s. 25 does not apply.

45. HENRY GUEST and his wife KATE GUEST are having problems in their marriage, HENRY having moved out of the family home to stay with his parents. HENRY and KATE have a son called DAMIAN, who is 13 years old, and they were married at the time of DAMIAN's birth. KATE decides to take DAMIAN on holiday for two weeks to Belfast as DAMIAN is doing a project on the city at school. KATE does not tell DAMIAN's father where they are going or seek his consent.

In relation to s. 1 of the Child Abduction Act 1984, does KATE GUEST commit an offence?

A Yes, as they were married at the time of the birth she must also obtain the consent of DAMIAN's father, HENRY.
B No, as KATE has not taken the child away without HENRY's consent for more than a month.
C Yes, because KATE did not communicate with HENRY even though his consent is not required.
D No, because KATE has not taken DAMIAN out of the United Kingdom.

46. DS EASTER a male officer and DC CUMMINGS a female officer have been part of the same CID crew for five years. DC CUMMINGS is qualified to the rank of sergeant and wishes to go to the next promotion boards. It will initially be down to DS EASTER to recommend her for promotion. One night after a good investigation they have both had too much to drink at the pub after work and DC CUMMINGS invites DS EASTER to her flat, to sleep it off. At the flat DS EASTER suggests that if DC CUMMINGS sleeps with him, her recommendation will be assured. This she does; however, because of the amount they have both drunk DS EASTER does not get a full erection and only manages to push against her vulva and does not ejaculate. They both fall asleep. At work the next day DS EASTER tells DC CUMMINGS that he cannot recommend her, as he is only allowed to recommend one person from his crew which will be DC WALKER.

Has DS EASTER committed rape in these circumstances?

A No, DS EASTER did not commit rape as no force or intimidation was made prior to the act and there was no full penetration.
B Yes, the offence of rape is made out in these circumstances.
C No, DS EASTER only broke a promise.
D Yes, but in the circumstances the offence would be attempted rape.

47. HANSON is found guilty at Sandford Crown Court of burglary of a dwelling house. He is sentenced to two years' imprisonment on 3 March 2011. He serves just over one year in prison, and is released on 4 April 2012.

In relation to possessing a firearm after conviction contrary to s. 21 of the Firearms Act 1968, which of the statements below is correct?

A Hanson can possess a firearm from 4 March 2016.
B Hanson can possess a firearm from 5 April 2017.
C Hanson can possess a firearm from 5 April 2015.
D Hanson is banned from possessing a firearm for life.

48. INGRAM and CUTHBERT both work at a local factory in the warehouse. In their morning break they go to the canteen and purchase a sandwich and drink and both sit in the canteen. CUTHBERT is a regular Sudoku fan and has a small book of these puzzles which he does in his break. INGRAM, on the other hand, reads the *Sun* newspaper. CUTHBERT is called away from the canteen by the manager to question him about his sick record. Whilst away, INGRAM has a look in CUTHBERT's Sudoku puzzle book and can see that CUTHBERT has nearly finished one of the puzzles so he fills in the last few needed numbers. CUTHBERT returns, moans about the manger taking him away from his break and picks up his Sudoku puzzle book and they return to work.

Which of the below statements is correct with regards to INGRAM's liability if any?

A INGRAM has no criminal responsibility for his actions.
B INGRAM has committed attempted theft, as the puzzle book was not removed by him.
C INGRAM has committed theft as he has treated the property as his own and for that period of time the priority rights of CUTHBERT were removed.
D INGRAM has appropriated the property in these circumstances.

49. TOM BARON is staying at his friend's address whilst his friend is on holiday. The house is in an area of heavily mixed race people. BARON has full use of the house and is allowed to bring his brother NIGEL to the house if he wishes. TOM and NIGEL, after a few beers at the local pub, are in the house watching a football match between their home team Wigan and Bournemouth in the play-offs for the FA Cup. During the match the Wigan defender ADOMAKO—a black player—makes a mistake allowing Bournemouth to score a goal. TOM shouts out 'You stupid black bastard; fuck off home to your mud hut'. This is shouted so loud that a West Indian couple passing the house hear what is said, however, this was not his intention.

In relation to using of words or behaviour or display of written materials contrary to s. 18 of the Public Order Act 1986 does BARON commit an offence?

A Yes, he commits the offence in these circumstances as racial hatred is likely to be stirred up.
B No offence is committed, as his response was in relation to a sporting event and s. 18 only applies to offences in a public place not a private dwelling.
C Yes, he commits the offence as another person is present in the dwelling and he is not the householder.
D No, as what was said was said in a dwelling and he was not aware that a person outside the dwelling would hear what was said.

50. KENT and KNOWLES have gone to the seaside for the day with some friends. They go for a drink in a pub and lose track of time and later that day they realise that their friends have gone home without them. KENT suggests that they steal a car in order to return home. KNOWLES agrees. KENT and KNOWLES go to a local supermarket and see WILSON loading his vehicle with shopping; they also note that the engine is running. KENT jumps into the driver's seat and KNOWLES gets in the vehicle, sitting in the front passenger seat. KENT initially starts to pull away; however, WILSON starts shouting and to shut him up KENT stops the car, puts the vehicle into reverse and backs up violently, killing WILSON. KENT and KNOWLES then drive off and dump the vehicle near home.

In relation to accessories for an offence, which of the following statements is correct?

A KENT would be responsible for the taking of the vehicle and the death of WILSON. However, KNOWLES would only be guilty of the taking of the vehicle, as this would not be classified as an 'unusual consequence'.
B Both KENT and KNOWLES would become equally guilty as soon as they enter a joint enterprise for the original offence.
C Both KENT and KNOWLES would be equally guilty as they had entered a joint enterprise and both were present at its commission; so KNOWLES by his mere presence is encouraging the crime, even though he does not communicate an encouragement.
D Both KENT and KNOWLES would be equally guilty as soon as they enter the car, as the joint enterprise has commenced.

51. ANDREWS and SMITH are driving around their estate when they see a Transit van with UK Mail on the side. They follow it for a while and realise that it is delivering goods to a variety of addresses and the boxes they see are marked with the company name of Amazon. ANDREWS and SMITH decide that they are going to steal from the van if they get the opportunity. The van turns down a cul-de-sac by some disused industrial units and parks up, and they can see smoke coming from the driver's side window; they realise the driver is having a crafty fag. They accelerate at high speed and screech to a halt in front of the van. The driver LAMB freezes to the spot; he is petrified when he sees ANDREWS and SMITH get out of the car. ANDREWS and SMITH just stare at the driver LAMB who looks away, throwing out his fag and winding up the window. ANDREWS and SMITH go to the rear of the vehicle and start yanking at the handle which is quite loose; they can see the packages inside, the handle breaks off but they cannot get into the vehicle. They then hear a police siren and may good their escape.

Which of the below is correct regarding the liability of ANDREWS and SMITH?

A They commit the offence of attempted theft.
B They commit the offence of attempted robbery.
C They commit the offence of vehicle interference.
D They commit the offence of criminal damage.

52. ANNE WELLS is a 14-year-old female and is at a camp site for the scouts and all the children have individual tents. The boys' tents are at the rear of the site and the girls' tents are near the front of the site. ANNE quite fancies one of the male scouts, HENRY BAKER, aged 16. WELLS decides that when the boys go swimming she will enter HENRY's tent and when he returns to get changed from his swimming gear she will take a picture of him naked on her mobile phone. WELLS enters BAKER's tent and hides in the corner behind his rucksack. BAKER returns and removes his swimwear and WELLS jumps out and attempts to take a picture. BAKER realises what is going on and stands there saying 'Go on then do your best'. However, there is no charge in the phone so no picture is taken and WELLS runs out of the tent.

In relation to s. 63 of the Sexual Offences Act 2003, trespass with intent to commit a relevant sexual offence, does WELLS commit an offence?

A No, as taking of indecent images is not a relevant sexual offence under s. 63.
B Yes, WELLS has trespassed on premises with intent to commit a relevant sexual offence; it does not matter that she did not take the photograph.
C No, it would not be an indecent image as BAKER is 16 or over and he had consented to the taking.
D Yes, but it would be an attempt as no image was taken; it does not matter that BAKER went on to consent, it is WELLS's intention on entry that is relevant.

53. HAWES is looking around an electrical shop and by the door sees on display a small iPod. He decides to steal this item, and when staff are distracted, he grabs the iPod, places it under his coat and runs out of the shop. The shop alarm is activated and the store detective, SMITH, gives chase. However, he loses sight of HAWES. A description is given to the police and MILES, a uniformed police officer, sees a person answering the description; however, it is not HAWES, it is another male, THOMAS. MILES approaches THOMAS and proceeds to caution and arrest him. Before he can do this, THOMAS shouts, 'Fuck off pig, I haven't done anything, you aren't arresting me.' He then punches MILES in the arm and attempts to run off. MILES overpowers THOMAS and arrests him.

In relation to s. 38 of the Offences Against the Person Act 1861 (assault with intent to resist arrest), which of the statements below is correct?

A THOMAS does not commit the offence as he was innocent of the original theft.

B THOMAS does commit the offence, even though he was innocent of the offence. However, there is no power of arrest under the 1861 Act.

C THOMAS does not commit the offence, as there is no power to arrest under the 1861 Act, and therefore it would be an unlawful arrest.

D THOMAS does commit the offence. However, he could use the defence that he was innocent of the original offence and therefore the officer was not in the execution of his duty.

54. Police have a drugs search warrant to search 12 Crook Close, the residence of GRAINGER. They set up observations to ensure he is on the premises. Police enter the premises at 07:00 hours and find half a kilo of heroin on the coffee table. However, GRAINGER is not there. Intelligence suggests that he is at his brother's house nearby. When they go to the brother's house they see GRAINGER walking down the road and arrest him at 08:10 hours for possession with intent to supply. During the search of GRAINGER they find a set of drug scales. GRAINGER is taken to the police station. Background checks reveal that GRAINGER's DNA (semen) was recovered from a rape victim two weeks earlier; he is further arrested for this offence. GRAINGER is interviewed and replies 'no comment' to all questions.

In relation to s. 36 of the Criminal Justice and Public Order Act 1994, which of the following is correct in relation to Special Warning GRAINGER in interview?

A GRAINGER can be special warned for the heroin, scales, and DNA.

B GRAINGER can be special warned for the heroin and scales, but he cannot be warned for the DNA.

C GRAINGER cannot be special warned for the heroin, scales, or DNA.

D GRAINGER can only be special warned for the scales.

55. LONG has been arrested for an offence of burglary and has agreed to stand on an ID parade.

To comply with PACE which of the below statements is correct with regards to the numbers required in an ID parade with one suspect.

A At least seven persons plus the suspect.
B Eight persons including the suspect.
C At least eight plus the suspect.
D Nine persons including the suspect.

56. GREY is unemployed and accepts a job as caretaker at a private girls' junior school. GREY has a fetish for young girls in white knickers. All the young girls wear a school skirt and blouse and all have to wear white briefs as part of the uniform. When the girls are in the playground at lunchtimes GREY positions himself so he can see the girls playing and in particular doing handstands against the refectory wall, which more often than not exposes their pants. During lunchtime a girl falls and scratches her knee and GREY goes to her assistance, and whilst applying first aid to her knee has a clear view up her skirt. A short time later, one of the teachers comes over and takes the girl to the first aid room. This has so excited GREY that he goes to the school potting shed and masturbates.

Which of the following statements is correct with regards to GREY committing an offence, contrary to s. 7 of the Sexual Offences Act 2003?

A GREY commits the offence when he observes the girls doing handstands.
B GREY does not commit the offence because he was not observed masturbating.
C GREY commits the offence when he touches the girl's knee and looks up her skirt.
D GREY does not commit the offence, as the touching was not sexual.

57. SUSAN MIDDLETON comes home from work at lunchtime and as she enters her house she becomes conscious that somebody is on the premises. MIDDLETON goes into the lounge area and can see two large men in her conservatory; she does not know them and they are removing the television from the wall. MIDDLETON reacts by locking the patio doors that lead to the conservatory, which totally imprisons the two men, and summoning the police believing the two men to be burglars. It transpires on police attendance that her husband had arranged for the two men to deliver a new television whilst she was at work as a surprise.

In relation to the offence of false imprisonment contrary to common law, which of the following statements is correct?

A MIDDLETON does not commit the offence as she has the defence that she was protecting her own property.
B MIDDLETON commits the offence of false imprisonment, as she intentionally restricted the two men's movements.
C MIDDLETON does not commit the offence as she was not present in the conservatory before imprisoning the two men.
D MIDDLETON commits the offence of false imprisonment, but in view of the fact that they were legitimate workers it would be a reckless false imprisonment.

58. FIONA, a 16-year-old female, lives with her step-brother PETER, aged 19 years, in the family household. Whilst her mother and his father are out one evening, she pleads with PETER to have sex with her as she feels embarrassed at school as all her friends have a greater knowledge of sex. PETER refuses.

In relation to s. 44 of the Serious Crime Act 2007 (intentionally encouraging or assisting an offence), does FIONA commit an offence in these circumstances?

A Yes, all the elements of intentionally encouraging an offence are present.
B No, as she is intentionally encouraging an offence created for her own protection.
C Yes, but as no sex took place it would be an attempt.
D No offence would be committed had PETER had sex with FIONA, as they would have both been consenting.

59. MASTERS has been arrested at his home address for an offence of burglary. Whilst searching his house under s. 32 of PACE you find undeveloped film in his bedside cabinet. He informs you that the undeveloped film shows indecent pictures of his half-sister aged 17, which she had consented for him to take, and which he was going to develop solely for his own use.

Is MASTERS guilty of an offence, contrary to s. 1 of the Protection of Children Act 1978?

A Yes, this Act and section cover possession of undeveloped film.
B No, he does not commit this offence, as she is over 16.
C Yes, but he would have the defence that she consented to the taking, even though she is under 18.
D No, undeveloped film is not covered by this offence.

60. DC ESSEX has just finished audio interviewing KITE for an offence of handling. KITE is represented by MANOR, his solicitor. When invited to sign the master seal KITE refuses, but MANOR, the solicitor, does sign the master seal.

In order to comply with Code E, para. 4.18 of PACE, which of the statements below is correct?

A An Inspector, or if not available, the custody officer should be called into the interview room to sign the seal.
B An Inspector should be called into the interview room to sign the seal.
C There is no need for the seal to be signed, as the solicitor has signed the seal, just for the officer present.
D The custody officer should be called into the interview to sign the seal.

61. MURRAY and MURRAY are brother and sister and aged 19 and 18 years respectively; they both know this to be the case. One evening whilst at home and having had a couple of drinks they have full consensual sex together, this only happens once on this occasion. Six months later this matter comes to the notice of the police and both are charged under s. 64 and s. 65 of the Sexual Offences Act 2003 respectively.

What is the maximum prison sentence that could apply to them both in these circumstances?

   A 6 months' imprisonment.
   B 12 months' imprisonment.
   C 2 years' imprisonment.
   D 5 years' imprisonment.

62. Victoria Shopping Mall has a Wishing Well placed at the entrance, and there is a sign indicating that the monies from the Wishing Well will be collected from time to time and given to a local charity for the benefit of deprived children. The Wishing Well is failing to attract as many donations as it is over three years old and looking a bit drab. The Mall proprietors decide that they will upgrade it. On emptying the Well they count the funds and there is a total of £1,006; they decide that the new Well will be much more attractive and will use £400 of the donations towards the upgrading, seeing this as overall assistance to the charity.

In relation to s. 5 of the Theft Act 1968 (obligations regarding another's property), has an offence been committed?

   A Yes, the proprietors have not dealt with the monies as intended.
   B No, as these are voluntary donations they are not covered by s. 5 of the 1968 Act.
   C Yes, but only if they had used all the funds; they had still dealt with the greater amount for the charity as intended.
   D No, because part of the funds were used to upgrade in an effort to increase donations.

63. MULLINS and HARDWICK go into the local bank; MULLINS is armed with an imitation firearm. There are two persons working on the bank tills, JONES and STAINES, and they are both sitting at two separate tills. MULLINS is standing opposite to STAINES, with his back to her and the gun against his chest. STAINES cannot see the gun. HARDWICK approaches JONES at the till. HARDWICK says to JONES, 'Look over there.' JONES looks over and can clearly see that MULLINS has a gun. HARDWICK then says, 'Handover £3,000 in cash or my mate will turn round and shoot that other cashier.' JONES freezes to the spot. HARDWICK nods to MULLINS, who turns and points the gun at STAINES. HARDWICK says, 'I'm not joking.' STAINES then hands over the cash.

At what point is the full offence of robbery first committed, contrary to s. 8 of the Theft Act 1968?

   A When HARDWICK makes the first demand for cash.
   B When MULLINS turns round and points the gun at STAINES.
   C When HARDWICK makes the second demand for the monies.
   D When STAINES hands over the cash.

64. Sergeant HUGHES is the custody officer at Bridge Street Police Station; he is proposing to bail FLINT for an offence of robbery. Sergeant HUGHES wishes to impose bail conditions on FLINT.

To comply with the bail conditions provided by s. 3A of the Bail Act 1976, which of the below conditions can Sergeant HUGHES not impose on FLINT?

A FLINT to reside at a bail hostel.
B FLINT to surrender his passport.
C FLINT to comply with curfew conditions.
D FLINT to provide a surety or security.

65. DEVLIN is a 38-year-old male and lives with his common-law partner ONIONS, who is a 36-year-old female. They have lived together for three years and DEVLIN has been the stepfather to ONIONS' daughter, GAIL. GAIL has now reached the age of 16 years, having been 13 years of age when he moved into their family home. Whilst her mother is out GAIL approaches DEVLIN and asks him if he will wash her back while she takes a bath. He is excited by this and agrees; following the bath they have consensual vaginal sex in her bedroom.

Has DEVLIN committed an offence in relation to s. 25 of the Sexual Offences Act 2003 (sexual activity with a family member)?

A No, as GAIL has consented, is over 16 years, and even though she was a family member, as a step-parent it ceases at the age of 16.
B No, for it to be an offence under this section, it must be a close blood relative.
C No, as GAIL is over 16 and he is not a family member for the purposes of this section.
D Yes, as GAIL is under 18, and he is her step-parent.

66. DC BLAKE has been authorised to set up covert operation and goes to DS DENTON for advice. The premises from which the observations are going to be made are from a private flat above a take-away Chinese. From the flat, officers will be able to identify persons in the supplying of drugs to young persons in the area. DC BLAKE wishes to know what has to be done to comply with the *Johnson* ruling.

Which of the below is the advice that DS DENTON should give DC BLAKE?

A An officer of at least the rank of Detective Constable inspects the observation point/premises before the observations start to check the full understanding of the occupiers and immediately prior to the trial the same officer informs the occupier the results of which it is proposed to give in evidence and that the occupiers are the same persons.

B An officer of at least the rank of Detective Constable inspects the observation point/premises before the observations start to check the full understanding of the occupiers and immediately prior to the trial an officer of at least the rank of Detective Sergeant informs the occupier the results of which it is proposed to give in evidence and that the occupiers are the same persons.

C An officer of at least the rank of Detective Sergeant inspects the observation point/premises before the observations start to check the full understanding of the occupiers and immediately prior to the trial an officer of at least the rank of Detective Inspector informs the occupier the results of which it is proposed to give in evidence and that the occupiers are the same persons.

D An officer of at least the rank of Detective Sergeant inspects the observation point/premises before the observations start to check the full understanding of the occupiers and immediately prior to the trial an officer of at least the rank of Detective Chief Inspector informs the occupier the results of which it is proposed to give in evidence and that the occupiers are the same persons.

67. It is an offence to be in possession of extreme pornographic images as laid out in ss. 63–67 of the Criminal Justice and Immigration Act 2008.

Which of the following would not be considered to be an extreme pornographic image?

A A moving image of a man having sex with a dead sheep.

B A moving image of a man having sex with what appears to be a dead woman, who is not in fact dead.

C A still image of a woman having oral sex on a dead dog.

D A still image of a man inserting a knife into a woman's vagina.

68. TONKS is a 15-year-old male who meets a girl, DAVIS, aged 12, at a local fair in the village. After a time they decide to go for a walk in the woods and partake in heavy petting. This arouses TONKS, who asks her if she wants sex, to which she consents. However, concerned she might be too young, TONKS asks her if she has had sex before, which she confirms and states she is 14. He encourages her to have oral sex with him.

In relation to s. 5 of the Sexual Offences Act 2003 (rape of a child under 13), does TONKS commit this offence?

A Yes, but he would have the defence that he believed her to be over the age of 13.
B No, under s. 5 the offence includes vaginal and anal intercourse only, and TONKS is under 16.
C Yes, this offence covers oral sex and DAVIS's consent is irrelevant.
D No, TONKS is under 18 and, even though DAVIS's consent is not true consent, and he believed her to be over 13, this would not make him guilty under this section.

69. RUTTER is having problems with her boss PATTERSON who has put her on an action plan to improve RUTTER's professional skills. RUTTER believes these are unjustified which they are not and therefore decides to cause PATTERSON anxiety or distress. RUTTER sends PATTERSON a false letter from a solicitor stating that PATTERSON is being taken to court for the noise her dog makes in the garden in a morning from a nearby neighbour. RUTTER also sends a text from an unidentified mobile phone stating that PATTERSON's daughter has been involved in a minor accident at school. RUTTER also puts dog faeces through PATTERSON's letterbox.

Considering the offences under s. 1(1) of the Malicious Communications Act 1988, which if any offences have been committed?

A None of the acts by RUTTER are covered by this legislation.
B RUTTER only commits the offence when she sends the false letter.
C RUTTER commits the offence when she sends the false letter and the text.
D RUTTER commits the offence on all three occasions.

70. DAVID JACOBS is an 18-year-old male and he fancies REBECCA LAMBERT aged 18 years. JACOBS decides that he is going to have sex with her whether she wants to or not. JACOBS knows that LAMBERT is not interested in him, but loves fast cars. One day JACOBS borrows his uncle's Porsche to impress LAMBERT which has the desired effect when he offers to give her a lift home one evening. They both get into the Porsche and JACOBS drives for several miles at very high speeds doing 60 and 70 miles an hour in 40 and 50 limits. LAMBERT enjoys the experience. JACOBS does not drive directly to LAMBERT's house but she does not mind this as she loves the fast driving. On a country road JACOBS turns off into a small copse and switches off the engine. JACOBS goes to grab LAMBERT but she has realised what's going on and gets out of the car and runs to the road and begins to flag down a passing vehicle. JACOBS panics and drives off.

Does JACOBS commit an offence in relation to s. 62 of the Sexual Offences Act 2003 (committing a criminal offence with intent to commit a sexual offence)?

   A Yes, he has committed dangerous driving with intent to commit a sexual offence.
   B No, as dangerous driving is not a criminal offence under s. 62.
   C Yes, but he would have had to have committed some sexual offence for the offence to be complete.
   D No, as LAMBERT has attained the age of consent and consented to the driving, and there was no kidnap offence, required for s. 62.

71. SHADRACK lives in student accommodation and as it is raining outside he picks up a coat belonging to NEWMAN—unbeknown to SHADRACK there is a knife in the inside pocket. He goes to a local sex shop to have a look at the pornographic DVDs. SHADRACK notices that there is no person at the counter. SHADRACK then goes behind the counter and through the door into the stock room to see if there is anything worth stealing. SHADRACK sees several metal handcuffs hanging on a hook. He decides to steal a pair of these and places them in his trouser pocket. SHADRACK continues to look round the store room to see if there is anything else worth stealing when he is approached by the owner BAINES. SHADRACK panics and throws the handcuffs at BAINES hitting him on the forehead causing a large cut and a fractured skull. BAINES falls to the floor and SHADRACK walks over to him and kicks BAINES several times in the chest. SHADRACK then leaves the shop.

At what point does SHADRACK first commit the offence of aggravated burglary?

   A When SHADRACK enters the store room with the knife in his coat pocket.
   B When SHADRACK steals the handcuffs.
   C When SHADRACK throws the handcuffs hitting BAINES on the forehead.
   D When SHADRACK kicks BAINES several times in the chest.

72. UNDERWOOD is in police detention and you wish to take footwear impressions for comparison against footprints found at the scene of the crime. UNDERWOOD refuses permission for these to be taken.

In relation to the provisions of the inclusion of s. 61A into the Police and Criminal Evidence Act 1984, which of the statements below is correct?

A UNDERWOOD has to be in police detention for a recordable offence and force can be used to remove the footwear on the authority of the custody sergeant.

B UNDERWOOD has to be in police detention for an indictable offence and force can be used to remove the footwear on the authority of the custody sergeant.

C UNDERWOOD has to be in police detention for a recordable offence and any constable removing the footwear can exercise force.

D UNDERWOOD has to be in police detention for an indictable offence and any constable removing the footwear can exercise force.

73. TRACEY and HEATHER are university students studying art. They have been made aware that there is a classical concert in the main theatre at the university for all students this evening but in principle mainly for those studying music. There are tickets for this venue, but the seats are not allocated, working on a first come, first served basis. The tickets are being handed out in the main foyer of the university that lunchtime although there is no cost for them. By the time they are released from morning studies, TRACEY and HEATHER miss out on the tickets. In the refectory at lunchtime they see others with tickets and HEATHER realises that she can duplicate the tickets on her computer, which she does that afternoon. TRACEY and HEATHER turn up to the concert with their tickets which are checked by music staff at the university and they are allowed admittance, seeing the whole concert.

Are TRACEY and HEATHER guilty of Obtaining Services Dishonestly contrary to s. 11 of the Fraud Act 2006?

A No, even though they made a false representation, the service, the concert was free.

B Yes, the offence is committed in full as they made a false representation and gained the service, the concert.

C HEATHER would be guilty as she made the false representation, the tickets; like all fraud crime it is conduct crime, not the result.

D They are both guilty of attempt in these circumstances as the concert is free.

74. TYRELL, a landlord, is in dispute with HALFORD, who lives in a house TYRELL rents to him. TYRELL arms himself with an air rifle and goes round to the house. The house has net curtains at the window and TYRELL cannot see if anybody is in the dwelling. He fires a pellet at the window, causing the glass to break. Unbeknown to TYRELL, HALFORD was standing in the room when the pellet was fired.

Does TYRELL commit an offence under s. 1(2) of the Criminal Damage Act 1971?

A Yes, TYRELL had intended to damage property and was reckless as to whether any life was endangered.

B No, TYRELL had a lawful excuse to damage his own property, and therefore this offence is incomplete.

C No, it is not the damage that has endangered the life, but the missile, so this offence is not committed.

D Yes, TYRELL cannot have a lawful excuse to damage property for this offence; however, it must be accompanied with intent to endanger life.

75. NELSON is an 18-year-old male and his new girlfriend is LENNON a 15-year-old female. They have been going out together for a couple of weeks. LENNON is very shy and knows very little about sex. NELSON decides that the only way he is going to be able to have sex with LENNON is to show her pictures of a pornographic nature to lower her inhibitions so he can achieve sexual gratification at a later date. NELSON at first shows LENNON cartoon still images of persons having sex. Then a day later he shows her moving cartoons of persons having sex. A week later as LENNON is now showing more interest, NELSON shows her mild porn acts of adults on the internet and NELSON believes that after this showing she will have sex with him. LENNON is not amused by this and tells him their relationship is over.

Considering the offence under s. 12 of the Sexual Offences Act 2003 (causing a child to watch a sex act) when if at all does NELSON first commit the offence?

A NELSON does not commit the offence as no sexual gratification was obtained whilst LENNON was watching the pictures.

B NELSON commits the offence when he showed her the internet porn as that was when he believed he would obtain sexual gratification.

C NELSON commits the offence when he shows the moving cartoon porn.

D NELSON commits the offence when he shows LENNON the first cartoon still image.

76. Under s. 33 of the Criminal Justice and Police Act 2001, a court is empowered to give an offender a travel restriction order for a drug trafficking offence. This is to prohibit them leaving the United Kingdom after their release from prison. They are guilty of an offence if they do not comply and they may have to surrender their passport.

Under s. 33 of the Criminal Justice and Police Act 2001, which of the statements below is the criteria for the court issuing such an order for a drug trafficking offender?

A Must have had a sentence imposed of at least three years, and then the restriction order is for a minimum of two years.

B Must have had a sentence imposed of at least four years, and then the restriction order is for a minimum of two years.

C Must have had a sentence imposed of at least three years, and then the restriction order is for a minimum of three years.

D Must have had a sentence imposed of at least four years, and then the restriction order is for a minimum of three years.

77. NICKLIN arms himself with an air pistol just in case somebody disturbs him. He goes to a local slaughterhouse in the cattle market late one evening. NICKLIN knows that there is no security at the market and he checks to see if any of the freezers have been left insecure containing the carcasses for delivery to the butchers the next day. He finds one of the freezers insecure, enters, and steals a half carcass of lamb.

Which of the statements below is correct with regards to the offence(s) committed by NICKLIN?

A NICKLIN has committed theft and possession of a firearm at the time of committing an indictable offence contrary to s. 17(2) of the Firearms Act 1968.

B NICKLIN has committed burglary only, as industrial freezers are premises for the purpose of burglary; but air weapons are not a weapon of offence for the purposes of aggravated burglary.

C NICKLIN has committed aggravated burglary in these circumstances as air weapons are included as a weapon of offence and industrial freezers are classed as premises.

D NICKLIN commits theft only, as industrial freezers are not premises and to commit an offence contrary to s. 17(2) of the Firearms Act 1968 the weapon has to be shown or used.

78. LEATHER is annoyed at the amount of coverage on the war in Iraq and, owing to the fact that British citizens were paying for the war, he believes that no more Muslims should be allowed into this country. He makes a banner out of an old bed sheet and paints on it 'No more Muslims to come here.' LEATHER parades his banner in the park near to the local mosque; however, he does not say anything. It is his intention to cause trouble in the local community.

Does LEATHER commit an offence under s. 18 of the Public Order Act 1986?

A No, for this offence it has to be in relation to nationality, not to religion.

B Yes, it was LEATHER's intention to stir up racial hatred; it can be for religion only.

C No, when displaying the banner LEATHER must communicate for the offence to be complete.

D Yes, it was LEATHER's intention to stir up racial hatred and it can be for religion or nationality.

79. SAMANTHA EVANS owns a local insurance agency and her business is falling on hard times. SAMANTHA EVANS approaches BEN EVANS, her brother, and asks him to hold up her shop on Friday when the takings will not have been banked and then she will be able to split the monies with him and balance the books. BEN EVANS is in a civil partnership with TERRY WILD and they live together. BEN tells TERRY that he has a job on to rob a shop and asks him to be the driver. TERRY is unaware that it is BEN's sister's premises that are going to be robbed. On the Friday morning when it is planned, TERRY's car won't start so the robbery does not go ahead.

Which of the following statements is correct with regards to an offence of Statutory Conspiracy contrary to s. 1 of the Criminal Law Act 1977?

A There is no conspiracy, as the crime has to be at least attempted and the car not being able to be started is too far removed for an attempt.

B Each person has to know of each person's involvement in the conspiracy for the offence to be complete.

C There is no conspiracy, as one is the intended victim and the other two are classed as spouses, even though it's a civil partnership.

D A conspiracy is committed, as each conspiracy is separate.

80. COOPER is an 18-year-old male and attends the local school. COOPER is very shy but is attracted to SHEAD, a 15-year-old male at his school, who has an interest in golf. COOPER finds out SHEAD's email address and sends him an email detailing how he would like to learn the game of golf and that he attends the same school and would SHEAD be interested in giving COOPER some basic lessons? SHEAD responds, stating that he would assist in teaching him golf and puts his mobile number on the return email. COOPER phones him and they have a discussion about basic skills. COOPER invites SHEAD round to his home on Saturday morning, knowing his parents will be out. COOPER intends to touch SHEAD intimately. SHEAD goes to COOPER's house on the Saturday morning; however, COOPER and SHEAD just talk, as COOPER is too embarrassed to do anything.

Considering s. 15 of the Sexual Offences Act 2003 (meeting a child following sexual grooming), does COOPER commit the offence?

A For COOPER to be guilty of the offence, sexual activity would need to have taken place.

B COOPER is guilty of the offence in these circumstances, even though SHEAD travelled to COOPER.

C COOPER is not guilty of the offence in these circumstances, as he did not travel with the intention of committing a relevant sexual offence and there were no sexual suggestions in the communications prior to the meeting.

D COOPER is not guilty in these circumstances, even though there does not need to be any sexual suggestion in the communications. COOPER must travel with the intention of committing a relevant sexual offence in any part of the world.

Blackstone's Police Investigators' Mock Examination Paper 2013

Answer Sheet

1 ⊏A⊐ ⊏B⊐ ⊏C⊐ ⊏D⊐	**31** ⊏A⊐ ⊏B⊐ ⊏C⊐ ⊏D⊐	**61** ⊏A⊐ ⊏B⊐ ⊏C⊐ ⊏D⊐
2 ⊏A⊐ ⊏B⊐ ⊏C⊐ ⊏D⊐	**32** ⊏A⊐ ⊏B⊐ ⊏C⊐ ⊏D⊐	**62** ⊏A⊐ ⊏B⊐ ⊏C⊐ ⊏D⊐
3 ⊏A⊐ ⊏B⊐ ⊏C⊐ ⊏D⊐	**33** ⊏A⊐ ⊏B⊐ ⊏C⊐ ⊏D⊐	**63** ⊏A⊐ ⊏B⊐ ⊏C⊐ ⊏D⊐
4 ⊏A⊐ ⊏B⊐ ⊏C⊐ ⊏D⊐	**34** ⊏A⊐ ⊏B⊐ ⊏C⊐ ⊏D⊐	**64** ⊏A⊐ ⊏B⊐ ⊏C⊐ ⊏D⊐
5 ⊏A⊐ ⊏B⊐ ⊏C⊐ ⊏D⊐	**35** ⊏A⊐ ⊏B⊐ ⊏C⊐ ⊏D⊐	**65** ⊏A⊐ ⊏B⊐ ⊏C⊐ ⊏D⊐
6 ⊏A⊐ ⊏B⊐ ⊏C⊐ ⊏D⊐	**36** ⊏A⊐ ⊏B⊐ ⊏C⊐ ⊏D⊐	**66** ⊏A⊐ ⊏B⊐ ⊏C⊐ ⊏D⊐
7 ⊏A⊐ ⊏B⊐ ⊏C⊐ ⊏D⊐	**37** ⊏A⊐ ⊏B⊐ ⊏C⊐ ⊏D⊐	**67** ⊏A⊐ ⊏B⊐ ⊏C⊐ ⊏D⊐
8 ⊏A⊐ ⊏B⊐ ⊏C⊐ ⊏D⊐	**38** ⊏A⊐ ⊏B⊐ ⊏C⊐ ⊏D⊐	**68** ⊏A⊐ ⊏B⊐ ⊏C⊐ ⊏D⊐
9 ⊏A⊐ ⊏B⊐ ⊏C⊐ ⊏D⊐	**39** ⊏A⊐ ⊏B⊐ ⊏C⊐ ⊏D⊐	**69** ⊏A⊐ ⊏B⊐ ⊏C⊐ ⊏D⊐
10 ⊏A⊐ ⊏B⊐ ⊏C⊐ ⊏D⊐	**40** ⊏A⊐ ⊏B⊐ ⊏C⊐ ⊏D⊐	**70** ⊏A⊐ ⊏B⊐ ⊏C⊐ ⊏D⊐
11 ⊏A⊐ ⊏B⊐ ⊏C⊐ ⊏D⊐	**41** ⊏A⊐ ⊏B⊐ ⊏C⊐ ⊏D⊐	**71** ⊏A⊐ ⊏B⊐ ⊏C⊐ ⊏D⊐
12 ⊏A⊐ ⊏B⊐ ⊏C⊐ ⊏D⊐	**42** ⊏A⊐ ⊏B⊐ ⊏C⊐ ⊏D⊐	**72** ⊏A⊐ ⊏B⊐ ⊏C⊐ ⊏D⊐
13 ⊏A⊐ ⊏B⊐ ⊏C⊐ ⊏D⊐	**43** ⊏A⊐ ⊏B⊐ ⊏C⊐ ⊏D⊐	**73** ⊏A⊐ ⊏B⊐ ⊏C⊐ ⊏D⊐
14 ⊏A⊐ ⊏B⊐ ⊏C⊐ ⊏D⊐	**44** ⊏A⊐ ⊏B⊐ ⊏C⊐ ⊏D⊐	**74** ⊏A⊐ ⊏B⊐ ⊏C⊐ ⊏D⊐
15 ⊏A⊐ ⊏B⊐ ⊏C⊐ ⊏D⊐	**45** ⊏A⊐ ⊏B⊐ ⊏C⊐ ⊏D⊐	**75** ⊏A⊐ ⊏B⊐ ⊏C⊐ ⊏D⊐
16 ⊏A⊐ ⊏B⊐ ⊏C⊐ ⊏D⊐	**46** ⊏A⊐ ⊏B⊐ ⊏C⊐ ⊏D⊐	**76** ⊏A⊐ ⊏B⊐ ⊏C⊐ ⊏D⊐
17 ⊏A⊐ ⊏B⊐ ⊏C⊐ ⊏D⊐	**47** ⊏A⊐ ⊏B⊐ ⊏C⊐ ⊏D⊐	**77** ⊏A⊐ ⊏B⊐ ⊏C⊐ ⊏D⊐
18 ⊏A⊐ ⊏B⊐ ⊏C⊐ ⊏D⊐	**48** ⊏A⊐ ⊏B⊐ ⊏C⊐ ⊏D⊐	**78** ⊏A⊐ ⊏B⊐ ⊏C⊐ ⊏D⊐
19 ⊏A⊐ ⊏B⊐ ⊏C⊐ ⊏D⊐	**49** ⊏A⊐ ⊏B⊐ ⊏C⊐ ⊏D⊐	**79** ⊏A⊐ ⊏B⊐ ⊏C⊐ ⊏D⊐
20 ⊏A⊐ ⊏B⊐ ⊏C⊐ ⊏D⊐	**50** ⊏A⊐ ⊏B⊐ ⊏C⊐ ⊏D⊐	**80** ⊏A⊐ ⊏B⊐ ⊏C⊐ ⊏D⊐
21 ⊏A⊐ ⊏B⊐ ⊏C⊐ ⊏D⊐	**51** ⊏A⊐ ⊏B⊐ ⊏C⊐ ⊏D⊐	
22 ⊏A⊐ ⊏B⊐ ⊏C⊐ ⊏D⊐	**52** ⊏A⊐ ⊏B⊐ ⊏C⊐ ⊏D⊐	
23 ⊏A⊐ ⊏B⊐ ⊏C⊐ ⊏D⊐	**53** ⊏A⊐ ⊏B⊐ ⊏C⊐ ⊏D⊐	
24 ⊏A⊐ ⊏B⊐ ⊏C⊐ ⊏D⊐	**54** ⊏A⊐ ⊏B⊐ ⊏C⊐ ⊏D⊐	
25 ⊏A⊐ ⊏B⊐ ⊏C⊐ ⊏D⊐	**55** ⊏A⊐ ⊏B⊐ ⊏C⊐ ⊏D⊐	
26 ⊏A⊐ ⊏B⊐ ⊏C⊐ ⊏D⊐	**56** ⊏A⊐ ⊏B⊐ ⊏C⊐ ⊏D⊐	
27 ⊏A⊐ ⊏B⊐ ⊏C⊐ ⊏D⊐	**57** ⊏A⊐ ⊏B⊐ ⊏C⊐ ⊏D⊐	
28 ⊏A⊐ ⊏B⊐ ⊏C⊐ ⊏D⊐	**58** ⊏A⊐ ⊏B⊐ ⊏C⊐ ⊏D⊐	
29 ⊏A⊐ ⊏B⊐ ⊏C⊐ ⊏D⊐	**59** ⊏A⊐ ⊏B⊐ ⊏C⊐ ⊏D⊐	
30 ⊏A⊐ ⊏B⊐ ⊏C⊐ ⊏D⊐	**60** ⊏A⊐ ⊏B⊐ ⊏C⊐ ⊏D⊐	

Marking instructions

- Mark like this ⊏A⊐
- Make no stray marks
- Please do **NOT** tick, cross, or circle

OXFORD
UNIVERSITY PRESS

Blackstone's Police Investigators'
Mock Examination Paper 2013

Pack 2

Contents

DO NOT OPEN THIS ANSWER PACK UNTIL YOU HAVE COMPLETED THE MOCK EXAM

Blackstone's Police Investigators' Mock Examination Paper 2013

Marking Instructions

Lay your answer sheet next to the marking matrix as shown below; you may find it useful to fold the answer sheet to do this. Starting with Question 1, compare your marked answer (in the example below this is 'C') with the correct answer given on the marking matrix. If the correct answer matches your marked answer put a '1' inside the white box on the relevant row. If it does not (see Question 2 below) put a '0'.

Please follow these instructions carefully to ensure accuracy. Marks ('1' or '0') should only be made in the white blank boxes (which indicate the subject area a question is related to)—please do not write anything in the grey boxes.

	Question No.	Correct Answer	Evidence	Property Offences	Assaults etc	Sexual Offences	Verification Question
1 ⊏A⊐ ⊏B⊐ ◀█ ⊏D⊐	1	C	1				
2 ⊏A⊐ ◀█ ⊏C⊐ ⊏D⊐	2	A		0			
3 ⊏A⊐ ◀█ ⊏C⊐ ⊏D⊐	3	B			1		
4 ⊏A⊐ ⊏B⊐ ◀█ ⊏D⊐	4	C				1	
5 ⊏A⊐ ⊏B⊐ ⊏C⊐ ◀█	5	A			0		
6 ⊏A⊐ ◀█ ⊏C⊐ ⊏D⊐	6	B			1		
7 ⊏A⊐ ⊏B⊐ ⊏C⊐ ◀█	7	D	1				

When you have marked the first 30 questions, add up the total for each column (Evidence; Property Offences; Assaults, Drugs, Firearms and Defences; and Sexual Offences) and enter the totals into the boxes marked A1, B1, etc. Then transfer these totals into the corresponding box ('A1', 'B1', etc) on the score sheet.

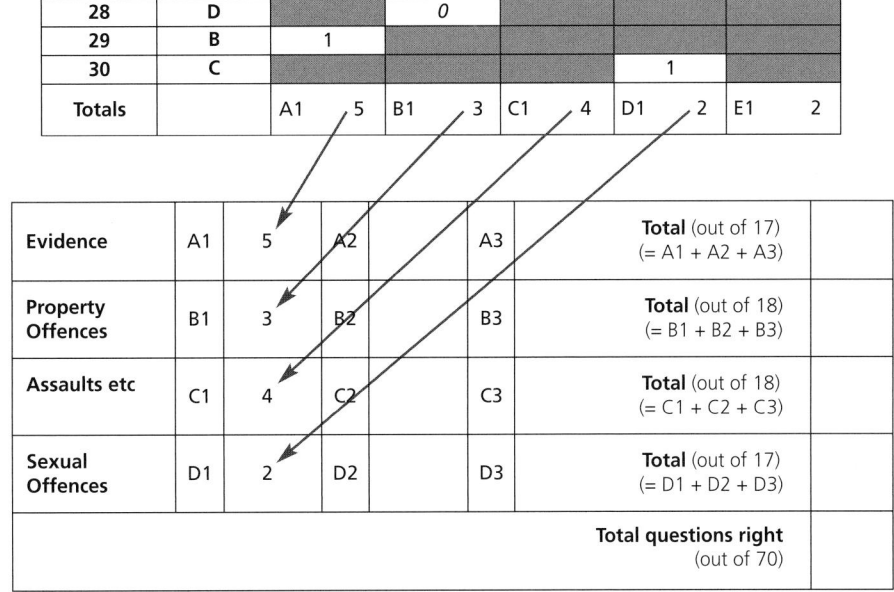

28	D		0			
29	B	1				
30	C				1	
Totals		A1 5	B1 3	C1 4	D1 2	E1 2

						Total	
Evidence	A1	5	A2		A3	**Total** (out of 17) (= A1 + A2 + A3)	
Property Offences	B1	3	B2		B3	**Total** (out of 18) (= B1 + B2 + B3)	
Assaults etc	C1	4	C2		C3	**Total** (out of 18) (= C1 + C2 + C3)	
Sexual Offences	D1	2	D2		D3	**Total** (out of 17) (= D1 + D2 + D3)	
						Total questions right (out of 70)	

Then do the same for Questions 31 to 60 and fill in boxes A2 to D2 on the score sheet, and finally Questions 61 to 80, which will enable you to fill in boxes A3 to D3 on the score sheet.

Total up A1 + A2 + A3, which will give you a score for Evidence. Then do the same for Property Offences, Assaults, etc, and Sexual Offences. You will then have a total for each subject area, which you can add up to reach a final total for the whole exam.

Compare your final total to the table underneath the score sheet, which will indicate whether or not you have passed the mock examination. The pass mark for the exam is 39.

Marking Matrix, Questions 1–30

Evidence	Answer	Evidence	Property Offences	Assaults, etc.	Sexual Offences	Verification Question
1	C					
2	A					
3	B					
4	C					
5	A					
6	B					
7	D					
8	A					
9	C					
10	D					
11	B					
12	A					
13	D					
14	C					
15	A					
16	B					
17	A					
18	C					
19	D					
20	B					
21	A					
22	C					
23	D					
24	B					
25	B					
26	C					
27	A					
28	D					
29	B					
30	C					
Totals		A1	B1	C1	D1	E1

Marking Matrix, Questions 31–60

Question No.	Correct Answer	Evidence	Property Offences	Assaults, etc.	Sexual Offences	Verification Question
31	B			✓		
32	D		✓			
33	A	✓				
34	C		✓			
35	C			✓		
36	B					✓
37	A			✓		
38	C					✓
39	D		✓			
40	B				✓	
41	D	✓				
42	C					✓
43	A		✓			
44	B	✓				
45	D			✓		
46	C				✓	
47	B					✓
48	D		✓			
49	D			✓		
50	A	✓				
51	B		✓			
52	A				✓	
53	B			✓		
54	D	✓				
55	C	✓				
56	D				✓	
57	A			✓		
58	B	✓				
59	D				✓	
60	A					✓
Totals		A2	B2	C2	D2	E2

Marking Matrix, Questions 61–80

Question No.	Correct Answer	Evidence	Property Offences	Assaults, etc.	Sexual Offences	Verification Question
61	C					○
62	A		○			
63	D		○			
64	A	○				
65	D				○	
66	D	○				
67	B				○	
68	C				○	
69	D			○		
70	A				○	
71	B		○			
72	C	○				
73	A		○			
74	C					○
75	D				○	
76	B			○		
77	C		○			
78	A			○		
79	C	○				
80	B				○	
Totals		A3	B3	C3	D3	E3

Score Sheet

(Please note that your score for verification questions is not included on this score sheet.)

Evidence	A1		A2		A3		**Total** (out of 17) (= A1 + A2 + A3)	
Property Offences	B1		B2		B3		**Total** (out of 18) (= B1 + B2 + B3)	
Assaults, etc.	C1		C2		C3		**Total** (out of 18) (= C1 + C2 + C3)	
Sexual Offences	D1		D2		D3		**Total** (out of 17) (= D1 + D2 + D3)	
							Total questions right (out of 70)	

Questions right	% score	Questions right	% score	Questions right	% score	Questions right	% score	Questions right	% score
1	1.429	15	21.429	29	41.429	43	61.429	57	81.429
2	2.857	16	22.857	30	42.857	44	62.857	58	82.857
3	4.286	17	24.286	31	44.286	45	64.286	59	84.286
4	5.714	18	25.714	32	45.714	46	65.714	60	85.714
5	7.143	19	27.143	33	47.143	47	67.143	61	87.143
6	8.571	20	28.571	34	48.571	48	68.571	62	88.571
7	10	21	30	35	50	49	70	63	90
8	11.429	22	31.429	36	51.429	50	71.429	64	91.429
9	12.857	23	32.857	37	52.857	51	72.857	65	92.857
10	14.286	24	34.286	38	54.286	52	74.286	66	94.286
11	15.714	25	35.714	39	55.714	53	75.714	67	95.714
12	17.143	26	37.143	40	57.143	54	77.143	68	97.143
13	18.571	27	38.571	41	58.571	55	78.571	69	98.571
14	20	28	40	42	60	56	80	70	100

Answer Booklet

1. Answer **C** — an 'intimate sample' means a dental impression or sample of blood, semen or any other tissue fluid, urine or pubic hair, or a swab taken from any part of a person's genitals or from a person's body orifice other than the mouth. Intimate samples may be taken if a police officer of the rank of inspector or above believes that such an impression or sample will tend to confirm or disprove the suspect's involvement in a recordable offence. Clearly, in the circumstances, the dental impression can be taken and it is an intimate sample. However, the sample of pubic hair would not indicate if MEARS was or was not responsible for the offence of murder so therefore could not be taken, making C the only correct option.

Investigators' Manual, para. 1.8.7

2. Answer **A** — A person is guilty of robbery if he steals and, immediately before or at the time of doing so, and in order to do so, he uses force on any person **or** puts or seeks to put any person in fear of being then and there subjected to force. KINSELLA and TARRANT are guilty of robbery with regards to the escalator incident, as the force can be used on ANY person, not necessarily the victim. TARRANT, with regards to CARTER, does not commit robbery because the force used was for another purpose, i.e. sexual assault.

Investigators' Manual, para. 2.4

3. Answer **B** — The qualifying triggers under s. 55 of the Coroners and Justice Act 2009 are:

- the defendant's fear of serious violence from the victim against the defendant or another identified person (this makes A and D incorrect as they are qualifying triggers);
- the defendant's loss of control was attributable to a thing or things done or said (or both) which constituted circumstances of an extremely grave character and caused the defendant to have a justifiable sense of being seriously wronged (this makes C incorrect as it is also a qualifying trigger).

Section 55(6) of the Coroners and Justice Act 2009 states that in determining whether the loss of self-control had a qualifying trigger:

- the defendant's fear of serious violence is to be disregarded to the extent that it was caused by a thing the defendant incited to be done or said for the purpose of providing an excuse to use violence;

- a sense of being seriously wronged by a thing done or said is not justifiable if the defendant incited the thing to be done or said for the purpose of providing an excuse to use violence;
- the fact that the thing done or said constituted sexual infidelity is to be disregarded.

This makes B the correct answer.

Investigators' Manual, para. 3.1.3.2

4. Answer **C** — A person (A) commits an offence if:
   - he intentionally touches a person (B);
   - the touching is sexual;
   - B does not consent to the touching; and
   - A does not reasonably believe that B consents.

'Touching' under s. 79(8) of the Sexual Offences Act 2003 is defined as:
   - with any part of the body;
   - with anything else;
   - through anything,

and in particular, touching amounting to penetration.

A is incorrect, as sexual gratification for crimes under the sexual offences act only applies to ss. 11 and 12 in your syllabus. Beware of this distracter; it is used in the real exam. B is incorrect as it does not have to be an intimate area touched. D is incorrect; the only offences in the sexual offences that aren't gender neutral are ss. 1 and 5 (rape and rape of a child under 13), when the offender has to be male. Whether KINNOCK is aware is irrelevant.

Investigators' Manual, para. 4.4.2

5. Answer **A** — The Firearms Act 1968, s. 16 states:

It is an offence for a person to have in his possession any **firearm** or **ammunition** with intent by means thereof to endanger life or to enable another person by means thereof to endanger life, whether injury is caused or not.

Therefore the only possible answer is A, as LENNON had an imitation firearm. This is a popular area for questioning in the exam as it does not cover imitation firearms, unlike ss. 16A, 17(1), 17(2), and 18. You will notice that the offence title has not been put in italics alongside the section. This is particular to this offence as it gives away too much information: 'Possessing a firearm with intent to endanger life'.

Investigators' Manual, para. 3.9.9.1

6. Answer **B** — Reference to the Manual will give the defined list, of which a vehicle registration document is not listed. This may seem an unfair question. The Forgery and Counterfeiting Act 1981 will have been on the NIE syllabus for three years and there is yet to be a question asked. It is just a matter of time. The legislation is quite complicated but once understood it is hard to write a question where the answer is not obvious, therefore checking your knowledge of what an instrument is under s. 5 and/or s. 8 is a likely source that could be tested.

Investigators' Manual, para. 2.6.11.5

7. Answer **D** — The relevant rank for Directed Surveillance is Superintendent or above; however, where it is not practical then an Inspector can authorise in urgent cases. In urgent cases a Superintendent may give oral authorisation. In urgent cases given orally by a Superintendent or authorised by an Inspector it will cease after 72 hours unless renewed. D is therefore the only correct option.

Investigator's Manual, para. 1.4.6.2

8. Answer **A** — The Sexual Offences Act 2003, s. 3 states:

A person (A) commits an offence if—

(a) he intentionally touches another person (B);
(b) the touching is sexual;
(c) B does not consent to the touching; and
(d) A does not reasonably believe that B consents.

'Touching'— s. 79(8) states that touching includes touching:

- with any part of the body;
- with anything else;
- through anything;

and in particular, touching amounting to penetration.

Touching for the purposes of an offence under s. 3 includes the touching of a person's clothing. Therefore, where a man approached a woman and asked, 'Do you fancy a shag?', grabbing at a pocket on her tracksuit bottoms as she tried to walk away, he was properly convicted of the s. 3 offence (*R v H* [2005] EWCA Crim 732). Therefore, from this test case the only option is A. B and D are incorrect because the offence is made out. C is incorrect, as sexual gratification is not part of the s. 3 definition.

Investigators' Manual, para. 4.4.2

9. Answer **C** — The Homicide Act 1957, s. 2 states:

(1)   A person (D) who kills or is party to the killing of another is not to be convicted of murder if D was suffering from an abnormality of mental functioning which—
      (a) arose from a recognised medical condition,
      (b) substantially impaired D's ability to do one or more of the things mentioned in subsection (1A) and
      (c) provides an explanation for D's acts and omissions in doing or being party to the killing.
(1A) Those things are—
      (a) to understand the nature of D's conduct;
      (b) to form a rational judgment;
      (c) to exercise self-control.
(1B) For the purpose of subsection (1)(c), an abnormality of mental functioning provides an explanation for D's conduct if it causes, or is a significant contributory factor in causing, D to carry out that conduct.
(2)   On a charge of murder, it shall be for the defence to prove that the person charged is by virtue of this section not liable to be convicted of murder.

(3) A person who but for this section would be liable, whether or as a principal or as accessory, to be convicted of murder shall be liable instead to be convicted of manslaughter.

(4) The fact one party to the killing is by virtue of this section not liable to be convicted of murder shall not affect the question whether the killing amounted to murder in the case of any other party to it.

TRANTER and FIELD were clearly acting in a joint enterprise therefore they are both equally guilty whether or not they pulled the trigger. TRANTER's recognised medical condition under s. 2 of the Homicide Act 1957 means he would be guilty of manslaughter in both cases. FIELD cannot use TRANTER's medical condition to reduce his liability even though a co-defendant, so therefore is guilty of the murder of both DAVIS and KYTE making C the correct option.

Investigator's Manual, para. 3.1.3.1

10. Answer **D** — Criminal conduct is most often associated with the *actions*; damaging or stealing property; injuring or deceiving others, but occasionally liability is brought about failure to act. Most of the occasions where failure or omission will attract liability are where a *duty to act* has been created. Such a duty can arise from a number of circumstances, the main ones being:

D Creating a dangerous situation.
U Under statute.
T Taken upon himself.
Y Young person.

PC EVERETT is under a duty of statue to act, making D the correct answer. He is not expected to put himself in harm's way but equally he cannot omit to do something; he cannot just look the other way (*R v Dytham* [1979] QB 722).

Investigators' Manual, para. 1.2.3

11. Answer **B** — PACE s. 32 states:
A constable may search an arrested person, in any case, where the person to be searched has been arrested at a place **other than at a police station** …
making B the only option. A is incorrect as s. 32 of PACE cannot be used in these circumstances.

DC CRUMP could have searched DANIELS under s. 1 (1) of PACE for a bladed and pointed weapon and then arrested him. The only power to search after arrest in these circumstances is the custody officer search under s. 54(1) para. 4.1 of PACE. Answers C and D are totally incorrect.

Investigators' Manual, para. 1.5.5.2

12. Answer **A** — PACE s. 55A allows a person who has been arrested and is in police detention to have an X-ray taken of them or an ultrasound scan to be carried out on them (or both) if:

(a) authorised by an officer of the rank of inspector or above who has reasonable grounds for believing that the detainee:
  (i) may have swallowed a Class A drug; and
  (ii) was in possession of that Class A drug with the intention of supplying it to another or to export; and
(b) the detainee's appropriate consent has been given in writing.

No force can be used.

Making A the correct answer.

Investigators' Manual, para. 1.6.25

13. Answer **D** — The Children Act 1989, s. 49 states:

    (1) A person shall be guilty of an offence if, knowingly and without lawful authority or reasonable excuse, he,
        (a) takes a child to whom this section applies away from a responsible person;
        (b) keeps such a child away from such a responsible person; or
        (c) induces or assists or incites such a child to run away or stay away from the responsible person.
    (2) This section applies in relation to a child who is—
        (a) in care;
        (b) the subject of an emergency protection order; or
        (c) in police protection.

Answers A, B, and C are incorrect as a child under this section is a child under the age of 18 years. Please note that the offence covers incite and therefore the offence would have been committed if JULIA had been in care and under 18.

Investigators' Manual, para. 4.6.5

14. Answer **C** — The Fraud Act 2006, s. 7 states:

    (1) A person is guilty of an offence if he makes, adapts, supplies or offers to supply any article—
        (a) knowing that it is designed or adapted for use in the course of or in connection with fraud or
        (b) intending it to be used to commit or assist in the commission of, fraud.

Both the credit card blanks and the data are articles as defined in the Fraud Act 2006 and BATERSBY does not have to be in possession of the articles to make the offer to supply, making C the only correct option. Since the increase in the pass mark for the National Investigators' Examination there has been an increase in the number of questions asked in relation to the Fraud Act so important revision required.

Investigators' Manual, para. 2.6.8

15. Answer **A** — The Sexual Offences Act 2003, s. 14 states:

    (1) A person commits an offence if—
        (a) he intentionally arranges or facilitates something that he intends to do, intends another to do, or believes another person will do, in any part of the world; and
        (b) doing it will involve the commission of an offence under any of sections 9 to 13.

Sections 9–12 cover offences against children when the offender is over 18. These offences are touching, causing or inciting, sexual activity in the presence of a child, and causing a child to watch a sexual act. Section 13 is a caveat to cover all ss. 9–12 when the offender is under 18 years of age. ADRIAN commits the offence when he facilitates (allows) JAMES and DIANE

WARNING: UNDER THE COPYRIGHT, DESIGNS AND PATENTS ACT 1988, PHOTOCOPYING THESE PAGES WITHOUT CONSENT MAY BE ILLEGAL
© Oxford University Press 2012

to use a bedroom together knowing that they are having sex. JULIE arranges when she books the holiday; sex does not have to have taken place and can be committed in any part of the world. Clearly this makes A correct and B, C, and D incorrect. Section 14 was designed to prevent the sex tourism trade; however, the definition goes beyond that.

Investigators' Manual, para. 4.5.5

16. Answer **B** — The Sexual Offences Act 2003, s. 75(2) states:

(a) any person was, at the time of the relevant act, or immediately before it began, using violence against the complainant or causing the complainant to fear that immediate violence would be used against him/her;

(b) any person was, at the time of the relevant act or immediately before it began, causing the complainant to fear that violence was being used, or that immediate violence would be used, against another person.

It is clear that for the offence of rape under s. 75 of the Sexual Offences Act 2003, that the violence used or threatened must be at the time, therefore as the threat was to the future it makes B the correct answer. Rape would have been committed, but under s. 74 of the Act which is the first limb of the definition of consent. It states that the person consents, if he or she agrees by choice and has the freedom and the capacity to make that choice; active consent rather than submission. SUE obviously in the circumstances did not have the freedom and capacity to make a choice. For the exam you must know ss. 74, 75 and 76 very well as they are all regularly tested and can be in a similar manner to the way that this question has been formulated.

Investigators' Manual, para. 4.3.4

17. Answer **A** — If the interview is to be with a juvenile, Code C, para. 11.16 gives guidance as to when interviews should take place at a juvenile's place of education. This should only be in exceptional circumstances and with the agreement of the principal or the principal's nominee. The juvenile's parent(s) or person(s) responsible for his/her welfare and the appropriate adult (if a different person) should be notified of the interview and be afforded time to attend. The principal or nominee can act as appropriate adult where waiting for an appropriate adult would cause unreasonable delay. This is not the case where the juvenile is suspected of an offence against his/her educational premises. Therefore A is the only option; as the damage is against the educational premises, the principal or nominee cannot act as the appropriate adult.

Investigators' Manual, para. 1.7.3

18. Answer **C** — The Theft Act 1968, s. 24, abbreviated points:

- Goods which have been stolen shall apply whether the stealing occurred in England or Wales or elsewhere. Making **A** incorrect.
- No goods shall be regarded as being continued to be stolen goods after they have been restored to the owner. Making D incorrect.
- It includes offences of blackmail and offences under the Fraud Act 2006 making B incorrect.
- Stolen goods include money which is dishonestly withdrawn from an account to which a wrongful credit has been made. Making C the correct answer.

It is well worth looking in detail at s. 24 of the Theft Act 1968 in your preparation for the exam; in order not only to answer questions similar to this but other questions that require this knowledge to answer them fully.

Investigators' Manual, para. 2.7.2

19. Answer **D** — It is an offence at common law falsely to imprison another person. It is an offence at common law to take or carry away another person without the consent of that person and without lawful excuse.

    Both of these offences can be committed intentionally or recklessly. Note that since the case of *R v Hendy-Freegard* [2007] EWCA Crim 1236 for the offence of kidnap, it is incomplete unless the victim is accompanied, making D the only possible answer. I doubt in the real exam that a single question would cover as much; however, this question is to ensure your knowledge is improved in preparation for the real exam.

    Investigators' Manual, paras 3.4 and 3.5

20. Answer **B** — The Anti-social Behaviour Act 2003, s. 1 states:

    (1) This applies to premises if a police officer not below the rank of Superintendent (the authorising officer) has grounds for believing—
        (a) that at any time during the relevant period premises have been used in connection with the unlawful use, production or supply of a class A controlled drug, and
        (b) that the use of the premises is associated with the occurrence of disorder or serious nuisance to members of the public.

    Relevant period means the period of three months ending with the day on which the authorising officer considers whether to authorise the issue of a closure notice in respect of the premises. Making D an incorrect option.

    Premises are defined as including any land or other place (whether enclosed or not) and any outbuildings which are or are used as part of the premises. This makes A and C incorrect.

    Note that it is immaterial whether any person has been convicted of any offence relating to use, production or supply, This information also makes A and D incorrect.

    Investigators' Manual, para. 3.8.12

21. Answer **A** — The Theft Act 1968, s. 4(3) states:
    A person who picks mushrooms growing wild on any land, or picks flowers, fruit or foliage from any plant growing wild on any land, does not (although not in possession of the land) steal what he picks unless he does it for reward or for sale or other commercial purpose.

    Unless FOSTER had the intent to pick the blackberries for commercial sale 'at the time of the picking', then the later intent to sell them does not arguably make the fruit property.

    The Theft Act, s. 4(4) states:

    Wild creatures tamed or untamed, shall be regarded as property; but a person cannot steal a wild creature not tamed nor ordinarily kept in captivity, or the carcase of any such creature, unless either it has been reduced into possession by or on behalf of another person and possession of it has not since been lost or abandoned, or another person is in the course of reducing it into possession.

    Therefore once a person has reduced a wild animal into possession (by trapping, capturing, or shooting it) a wild animal can be stolen, the actions of JOHNSON, making A the correct answer. B is incorrect as the rabbit is property. C is incorrect as the blackberries are not property. D is incorrect as the blackberries do not become property when FOSTER sells them.

Investigators' Manual, para. 2.1.5

22. Answer **C** — The Proceeds of Crime Act 2002, s. 329 states:
A person commits an offence if he—

(a) acquires criminal property;
(b) uses criminal property;
(c) has possession of criminal property.

An additional defence exists under s. 329(2)(c), which states that a person will not commit the offence if he acquired or used or had possession of the property for adequate consideration. The effect of the defence is that persons, such as tradesmen, who are paid for ordinary consumable goods and services in money that comes from crime, are not under any obligation to question the source of the money, making C the correct answer.

Investigators' Manual, para. 2.8.6

23. Answer **D** — The actus reus needed to prove assault is an act which caused the victim to apprehend the immediate infliction of unlawful force. However, words can also negate an assault (*Tuberville v Savage* (1669) 1 Mod R3). In this type of assault the defendant is making a *hypothetical* threat and is really saying 'If it weren't for the existence of certain circumstances, I would assault you'. Making D the correct option.

Investigators' Manual, para. 3.2.2.4

24. Answer **B** — A person (A) commits an offence if:

- he intentionally penetrates the **vagina** or **anus** of another person (B) with a part of his body or anything else;
- the penetration is sexual;
- B does not consent to the penetration; and
- A does not reasonably believe that B has consented.

Therefore A and D are incorrect as the definition does not include the **mouth**. C is incorrect as the penetration can be with a body part or anything else, inserted into the vagina or anus. Note also that this offence is gender neutral.

Investigators' Manual, para. 4.4.1

25. Answer **B** — A person can be remanded into police custody. The Magistrates' Courts Act 1980 states:

- for a period not exceeding three days (24 hours for a person under 17 (s. 23(14) of the Children and Young Persons Act 1969) (s. 128(7)));
- for the purpose of enquiries into offences (other than the offence for which he/she appears before the court) (s. 128(8)(a));
- as soon as the need ceases he/she must be brought back before the magistrates (s. 128(8)(b));

- the condition of detention and periodic review apply as if the person was arrested without warrant on suspicion of having committed an offence (s. 128(8)(c) and (d)).

This remanding to custody is referred to in general terms as the three-day lie down: note that it was converted to hours in this question, a point to remember when answering some questions in the NIE.

Investigators' Manual, para. 1.9.10

26. Answer **C** — The Offences Against the Person Act 1861, s. 18 states:
    Whoever shall unlawfully and maliciously by any means whatsoever wound or cause any grievous bodily harm to any person with intent to do some grievous bodily harm to any person, or **with intent to resist or prevent the lawful apprehension** or detainer of any person, shall be guilty of a felony.

    Officers are aware that grievous bodily harm caused with intent is an offence under s. 18; e.g. some person stabbing some other person. I have highlighted the part of the definition that is required to achieve the correct answer for this question. The word maliciously means *recklessly* so CHANDLER has maliciously committed grievous bodily harm with INTENT to resist apprehension.

    Investigators' Manual, para. 3.2.12

27. Answer **A** — Section 8 of the Sexual Offences Act 2003 is identical to s. 4 of the Act except that **the** victim is under 13 and it includes inciting.

    This is covered in the keynote area of the Manual and is missed sometimes when revising. Note also that the title of definition in the question was not given; this is not uncommon when its title gives away too much information.

    The specific offence is of causing or *inciting* a child under 13 to engage in sexual activity (s. 8). It is important to remember that an individual can commit the offence of incitement even if the activity he/she is encouraging etc. does not take place. In *R v Walker* [2006] EWCA Crim 1907, the Court of Appeal held that s. 8 created two offences: (i) intentionally causing, and (ii) intentionally inciting a child under 13 to engage in sexual activity.

    Investigators' Manual, para. 4.4.3

28. Answer D — DANIELS has permission to be in the house so whilst he is in the house and he takes **anything** it can only be theft, unless he had identified the property to steal the day before and re-entered the house with that intent to steal, he would then commit a s. 9(1)(a) burglary. This also applies when he makes the decision in the hallway to re-enter the kitchen to break the window to make it look as though a burglary has taken place. When he crosses the threshold to the kitchen with that intent he becomes a trespasser and therefore guilty of burglary (s. 9(1)(a)). The taking of the money and the iPhone are thefts because at the time of the thefts DANIELS was not a trespasser.

    Investigator's Manual, para. 2.2.1

29. Answer **B** — A person is guilty of fraud if he is in breach of any of the sections listed in s. 1(2) of the Fraud Act 2006, one of which is fraud by false representation. It is apparent that NOBLE has made a false representation; however, the offence is complete once the false

representation is made, making A, C, and D incorrect. This has similarities to blackmail, i.e. once the unwarranted demand is made, the offence is complete.

Investigators' Manual, para. 2.6.3

30. Answer **C** — The Sexual Offences Act 2003, s. 4 states:

(1) A person (A) commits an offence if—
    (a) he intentionally causes another person (B) to engage in an activity;
    (b) the activity is sexual;
    (c) B does not consent to the activity; and
    (d) A does not reasonably believe B consents.

The activity must be sexual (see para. 4.2.1), what a reasonable person would believe to be sexual. The first sexual activity against BANNER is the kissing, making C the correct answer.

Investigators' Manual, para. 4.4.3

31. Answer **B** — The Child Abduction Act 1984, s. 2 states:
A person commits an offence if without lawful authority or reasonable excuse, he takes or detains a child under the age of 16—

(a) so as to remove him from the lawful control of any person having lawful control of the child; or

(b) so as to keep him out of the lawful control of any person entitled to lawful control of the child.

Defences:

(a) where the father and mother of the child in question were not married to each other at the time of his birth—
    (i) that he is the child's father; or
    (ii) that, at the time of the alleged offence, he believed, on reasonable grounds, that he was the child's father; or

(b) that, at the time of the alleged offence, he believed that the child had attained the age of 16.

A is incorrect as the offence is not one of strict liability. C is incorrect as the wording is similar to that of an old defence of USI (unlawful sexual intercourse) predating the Sexual Offences Act 2003 and D is incorrect as this wording applies to s. 1 of the Child Abduction Act 1984 making B the correct answer.

Investigator's Manual, para. 3.3.3

32. Answer **D** — A person commits an offence who, without lawful excuse, destroys or damages any property belonging to another intending to destroy or damage any such property or being reckless as to whether any such property would be destroyed or damaged. It is not an offence to damage your own property (making A and C incorrect), unless there are aggravating circumstances. (Making B incorrect.) Even if the intention in doing so is to carry out a further offence, such as a fraudulent insurance claim, this fact does not make it an offence under

s.1(1) of the Criminal Damage Act 1971 (*R v Denton* [1981] 1 WLR 1446). Making D the correct answer.

Investigators' Manual, para. 2.9.2.6

33. Answer **A** — For a person arrested outside England and Wales the relevant time starts at the time he first arrives at a police station in the police area where the matter is being investigated or 24 hours after he first entered England or Wales, whichever is the earliest. Therefore B is incorrect as he arrived in a force area police station prior to the station where it was being investigated. C is incorrect as it is not the police area in which the matter is being investigated and HENSON was not questioned about the offence. D is incorrect as this time only applies after 24 hours have elapsed, if he has not arrived at the police station in the force area where the offence is being investigated. Make sure you learn this area of PACE, as it is a very popular type of question.

Investigators' Manual, para. 1.6.16.1

34. Answer **C** — The Theft Act 1968, s. 27(3) states:

Where a person is being proceeded against for handling stolen goods (but not for any offence other than handling stolen goods), then at any stage in the proceedings, if evidence has been given of his arranging to have in his possession the goods subject of the charge, or of his undertaking or assisting in their retention, removal, disposal, or realisation, the following evidence shall be admissible for the purpose of proving that he knew or believed the goods to be stolen goods—

(a) evidence that he has had in his possession, or has undertaken or assisted in the retention, removal, disposal, or realisation of, stolen goods from any theft taking place not earlier than 12 months before the offence charged; and

(b) (provided that seven days' notice in writing has been given to him of the intention to prove the conviction) evidence that he has within the last five years preceding the date of the offence charged, been convicted of theft or handling stolen goods.

C in these circumstances is the only option. Owing to the fact it is hard to prove 'knowing or believing', s. 27 allows for the admissibility of previous misconduct. However, the overriding factor is that they cannot be charged with any other offence. This makes A, B, and D incorrect.

Investigators' Manual, para. 2.7.7

35. Answer **C** — The reason for this question is to highlight, within the revision programme, the need to know the CPS charging standards for assaults and grievous bodily harm.

Scratches are the injuries sustained for a s. 39 (Criminal Justice Act 1988) offence not a s. 47, offence therefore making A and D incorrect.

Multiple bruising is a charging standard for s. 47 and so too is the cutting of hair without consent. Even though the hair is medically dead tissue, it falls into the category of 'bodily harm' (*DPP v Smith (Ross Michael)* [2006] EWHC 94 (Admin)).

Investigators' Manual, para. 3.2.11

36. Answer **B** — The Firearms Act 1968, s. 17 states:

(1) It is an offence for a person to make or attempt to make any use whatsoever of a firearm or imitation firearm with the intent to resist or prevent the **lawful arrest** or detention of himself or another person.

NELSON does not have to be in possession of the firearm or imitation firearm making D incorrect. C is incorrect as the offence applies to imitation firearms. B is correct as it has to be a lawful arrest. In these circumstances an indictable offence has not been committed so the security guard has no power to arrest, making A incorrect.

Investigators' Manual, para. 3.9.9.3

37. Answer **A** — The Domestic Violence, Crime and Victims Act 2004, s. 5 states:
A person ('D') is guilty of an offence if—

(a) a child or vulnerable adult ('V') dies as a result of the unlawful act of a person who—
  (i) was a member of the same household as V; and
  (ii) had frequent contact with him;
(b) D was such a person at the time of the act;
(c) at that time there was significant risk of serious physical harm being caused to V by the unlawful act of such a person; and
(d) either D was the person whose act caused V's death or—
  (i) D was, or ought to have been, aware of the risk mentioned in paragraph (c);
  (ii) D failed to take such steps as he could reasonably have been expected to take to protect V from risk; and
  (iii) the act occurred in circumstances of a kind that D foresaw or ought to have foreseen.

It will be necessary to prove that the child or vulnerable person dies as a *result of an unlawful act*. 'Act' in these circumstances includes omissions: failure to feed the child. This makes B incorrect. (See DUTY for responsibilities of children, para. 1.2.3, re omissions.) No prosecution can be brought under s. 5 of a child under the age of 16 years unless they are the parent, and even in those circumstances there are restrictions on the steps they could reasonably have taken under that age. This makes C incorrect. D is incorrect as s. 5 is about persons living in the same household as the victim at the time of the death, not whether they are the parent, resulting in the death of a child or vulnerable adult.

Investigators' Manual, para. 3.1.6

38. Answer **C** — Section 5(1) and (1A) of the Firearms Act 1968 contains the full list of Prohibitive Weapons and use and possession is authorised by the Secretary of State making C the correct answer. This paragraph including the exceptions for prohibitive weapons is important revision. Although there may only be two or three questions in the NIE on firearms, this area is questioned quite regularly.

Investigators Manual, para. 3.9.4.1

39. Answer **D** — The roped off area is 'part of a building' for the purpose of burglary making A incorrect. B is incorrect as on entry LANE was going to TWOC the vehicle, not a trigger offence

for burglary. C is incorrect as he had entered before intending to commit the damage. D is correct because having entered part of a building as a trespasser he has stolen.

Investigators' Manual, para. 2.2.2

40. Answer **B** — The Sexual Offences Act 2003, s. 61 states:

(1) A person commits an offence if he intentionally administers a substance to or causes a substance to be taken by another person (B)—
    (a) knowing that B does not consent and
    (b) with the intention of stupefying or overpowering B, so as to enable any person to engage in a sexual activity that involves B.

FLOWERS had consented to the taking, and even though the definition is any substance for stupefying etc. has to be taken, it is without the knowledge of the victim. Therefore in this case ROGERS would have needed to 'spike' FLOWERS's drink by adding another substance, i.e. vodka or a drug. This is a preparatory offence so no act had to take place.

Investigators' Manual, para. 4.7.3

41. Answer **D** — The disclosure provisions of the Criminal Procedure and Investigations Act 1996 set out the retention periods for case material.

Where a person has been convicted, all material which may be relevant must be retained at least until:

- the person is released from custody or discharged from hospital in cases where the court imposes a custodial or hospital order;
- in all other cases, for six months from the date of conviction.

If a person is released from the custodial sentence or discharged from hospital earlier than six months from the date of conviction, material must be retained for at least six months from the date of conviction. Therefore B is incorrect as it cannot be disposed of on release, and furthermore A is incorrect in this regard and the three months served. C is incorrect not only on lengths but also the fact that custodial sentences and hospital orders do not have different rules. D is therefore correct.

Investigators' Manual, para. 1.10.7

42. Answer **C** — The issue of transferred mens rea, which is what the doctrine amounts to, can be important in relation to the liabilities of accessories. If the principal's intentions (DUNN) are to be extended to an accessory (ANDREWS), it must be shown that those intentions were contemplated or accepted by that person at the time of the offence, or they were transferred by this doctrine. Owing to the fact that there was an incitement to assault some agreed person and its execution resulted in the assault of another, then it would apply to the accessory. This would not apply if DUNN had just decided to assault another person. This makes A, B, and D incorrect.

Investigators' Manual, para. 1.1.5

43. Answer **A** — The Proceeds of Crime Act 2002, s. 340(4) states that it is immaterial:

- who carried out the criminal conduct;
- who benefited from it;
- whether the conduct was before or after the passing of the Act.

This offence applies to the thief too, not as with handling which states '*otherwise in the course of stealing*'. It does not matter that the crime was before the commencement of the 2002 Act.

The mens rea for criminal property and all three offences under the 2002 Act is knowing or *suspecting*, not as with handling (*knowing or believing*) (*R v Da Silva* [2006] EWCA Crim 1654).

B is incorrect as it excludes FULLER. C is incorrect as it excludes TRANTER and D is incorrect as it is irrelevant that the offences were committed before the commencement of the 2002 Act, making A the correct answer.

Investigators' Manual, paras 2.8.2 and 2.8.4

44. Answer **B** — The Criminal Justice and Public Order Act 1994, s. 25 provides only when bail can be given in **exceptional circumstances**. Section 25 lists to which offences this applies; basically, murder, attempted murder, manslaughter, and serious sexual offences (ss 1 to 8 but not including 3 or 7) if a person has been convicted before of any one of the offences and then commits any other offence in the list and is charged. Note the exception: if the first offence was manslaughter or culpable homicide and the offender was not given a custodial sentence, then s. 25 does not apply.

Investigators' Manual, para. 1.9.5

45. Answer **D** — The Child Abduction Act 1984, s. 1(1) states: a person connected with a child under the age of 16 commits an offence if he takes or sends the child out of the United Kingdom without the appropriate consent. So for the offence to be committed the child must be taken out of the United Kingdom. Clearly KATE has not done this as Belfast is part of the United Kingdom, making D the only option. Make sure you revise when permission is required and the defences to s. 1 of the Child Abduction Act 1984, as this is a popular subject in the National Investigators' Examination.

Investigators' Manual, para. 3.3.1

46. Answer **C** — The Sexual Offences Act 2003, s. 76 which explains the conclusive presumptions about consent, that apply to offences to ss. 1–4. These presumptions are: (a) intentionally deceiving the complainant as to the nature or purpose of the act; (b) intentionally inducing the complainant to consent to the relevant act by impersonating a person known personally to the complainant. DC CUMMINGS knew what the act of sex was therefore she was not deceived into the nature or purpose of the act (sex). So the issue of rape does not occur; DS EASTER just broke a promise, this makes A, B and D incorrect.

There is no need for the defendant to ejaculate and the Sexual Offences Act 2003 does not deal with penetration to the slightest degree as in the previous Act; however, references to include body parts does, so pushing against the vulva in other circumstances would be rape not attempted rape.

47. Answer **B** — The Firearms Act 1968, s. 21 provides that any person who has been sentenced to:

- custody for life; or
- preventive detention, imprisonment, corrective training, youth custody, or detention in a youth offender institution for three years or more

must not at any time, have a firearm or ammunition in his/her possession. Section 21 goes on to provide that any person who has been sentenced to imprisonment, etc. for three months or more but less than three years must not have a firearm or ammunition in his/her possession at any time before the end of a five-year period beginning on the date of his/her release, making B correct and A, C, and D incorrect.

Investigators' Manual, para. 3.9.11

48. Answer **D** — The Theft Act 1968, s. 3 states:

(1) Any assumption by a person of the rights of an owner amounts to an appropriation, and this includes, where he has come by the property (innocently or not) without stealing it, any later assumption of a right to it by keeping or dealing with it as the owner.

INGRAM has treated the property as his own when he filled in the Sudoku puzzle for that period of time. This does not amount to theft as it is only one element of the definition of theft. Making D the correct answer. In the actual exam, the breaking down of the elements of a definition to check your knowledge of the whole is a regular occurrence and in particular the elements of theft.

Investigators' Manual, para. 2.1.4

49. Answer **D** — The Public Order Act 1986, s. 18 states:

(1) A person who uses threatening, abusive or insulting words or behaviour, or displays any written material which is threatening, abusive or insulting is guilty of an offence if—
    (a) he intends to stir up racial hatred, or
    (b) having regard to all the circumstances racial hatred is likely to be stirred up.

There is however, a defence under s. 18(4).

In proceedings for an offence under this section it is a defence for the accused to prove that he was inside a dwelling and had no reason to believe that the words or behaviour used, or the written material displayed, would be heard or seen by a person outside that or any other dwelling.

This clearly makes D the correct answer. Sections 18 and 19 of the Public Order Act 1986 are regularly tested in the exam so some revision is required on this subject area.

Investigators' Manual, para. 3.7.12

50. Answer **A** — If an accessory is present at the scene of a crime when it is committed, his/her presence may amount to *encouragement*, which would support a charge of aiding and

abetting. However, mere presence at the scene of a crime will not usually be enough evidence of guilt (*R v Coney* (1882) 8 QBD 534).

For this question we need to consider:

- the nature and extent of the offence that was agreed upon and contemplated by the two of them when they set out on their joint enterprise.

Did *the* accessory realise:

- that the principal might kill someone;
- that, when killing, the principal might have the intention to kill; or
- an intention to cause grievous bodily harm?

If they had agreed to violently assault a person then one had produced a knife, the stabbing would be an 'unusual consequence' arising from the execution of that enterprise.

B is incorrect as it does not just apply at the beginning of the enterprise. C is incorrect as KNOWLES' mere presence is not enough in these circumstances, and D is incorrect as again it is more than just when the commission of the offence takes place, making A the correct answer.

Investigators' Manual, para. 1.2.6.2

51. Answer **B** — This is the type of question you can come across in the real examination or similar to it or in the sexual offences legislation. You can make a case for all the options to be correct, however, you have to decide which is the most correct. Part of the definition of robbery under s. 8 of the Theft Act 1968 states:

Puts or seeks to put any person in fear of being then and there subjected to force.

It is clear from the question that LAMB the driver was put in fear and therefore you have an attempted robbery, it being the most appropriate charge and the more serious offence.

Investigators' Manual, para. 2.4

52. Answer **A** — The Sexual Offences Act, s. 63 states:
A person commits an offence if:

- he is a trespasser on any premises;
- he intends to commit a relevant sexual offence on the premises; and
- he knows that, or is reckless as to whether, he is a trespasser.

Premises include a structure or part of a structure and include a tent, vehicle, or vessel, or other temporary structure, or moveable structure. A is correct as a 'relevant sexual offence' as explained at s. 62 in the Manual applies and does not cover trespass with intent, with regards to offences under the Protection of Children Act 1978 which is the taking of indecent images.

Investigators' Manual, paras 4.5.8 and 4.7.2

53. Answer **B** — The Offences Against the Person Act 1861, s. 38 states:
Whoever…shall assault a person with intent to resist or prevent the lawful apprehension or detainer of himself or of any other person for any offence, shall be guilty of a misdemeanour …

- triable either way;
- two years' imprisonment.

This may not seem a fair question. However, in the exam these are not uncommon ways of testing your knowledge. There is no power of arrest as it is not necessary to have one, as you arrest for the original offence, assuming that the person was acting within their powers. The officer, even though wrong, has the power to arrest on suspicion of theft. This would cover store detectives, benefit agency staff, and custody assistants, assuming they had the lawful power in the circumstances.

Once the lawfulness of the arrest is established, the state of mind necessary is an intention to resist/prevent that arrest. It is irrelevant whether or not the person arrested had actually committed an offence. A belief in one's own innocence, however genuine or honestly held, cannot afford a defence under s. 38 (*R v Lee* [2000] Crim LR 991). A and C are incorrect as he does commit the offence, and D is incorrect as being innocent is irrelevant and the execution of his duties is not relevant to this offence. However, check assaults on police in s. 89 of the Police Act 1996 as there is an overlap between the two offences. B, therefore, is the correct answer.

Investigators' Manual, paras 3.2.14.1 and 3.2.14.3

54. Answer **D** — Section 36 of the Criminal Justice and Public Order Act 1994 states:

(1) Where—
    (a) a person is arrested by a constable and there is—
       (i) on his person; or
      (ii) in or on his clothing or footwear; or
     (iii) otherwise in his possession; or
     (iv) in any place in which he is at the time of his arrest,

any object, substance or mark, or there is any mark on any such object; and

    (b) that or another constable investigating the case reasonably believes that the presence of any object, substance or mark may be attributable to the participation of the person arrested in the commission of an offence specified by the constable.

Let's consider what can be special warned.

The heroin cannot be special warned for because at the time of GRAINGER's arrest it was in police possession. (Had he been at the house or the arrest made prior to entering, then he could have been special warned.)

He can be special warned for the scales as they are in his possession at the time of the arrest.

He cannot be special warned for the DNA as he and it are not at the scene and, although a substance, it is not otherwise in his possession. It is about good evidence, not necessarily best evidence. Fingerprint and DNA only apply to Special Warnings if the DNA or the fingerprint is at the scene and so is the suspect.

Therefore only D can be the right answer.

This particular question covered more scenario alternatives than you will see in the real exam but this is for you to also understand the necessary concepts of the legislation.

Investigators' Manual, para. 1.7.2.3

55. Answer **C** — The identification parade shall consist of at least eight people (in addition to the suspect). If there are two suspects of similar appearance on the same identification parade then at least 12 people (in addition to the suspects).

Investigators' Manual, para. 1.8.9 C9

56. Answer **D** — The Sexual Offences Act 2003, s. 7 is not listed in the Manual as a full definition but it is referred to in the keynote area, and has a direct relation to s. 3 (sexual touching). For s. 7, if the victim is a child under the age of 13, you simply have to prove intention, sexual touching, and the child's age. Therefore to answer this question fully you also need to understand the definition of 'sexual'.

Section 78 provides *that* penetration, touching, or any other activity will be sexual if a reasonable person would consider that:

- whatever its circumstances or any other person's purpose in relation to it, it is sexual by its very nature, or
- because of its nature it *may* be sexual and because of the circumstances or purpose of any person in relation to it, it is sexual.

Fetishes are not covered by the Act so A is incorrect. A reasonable person seeing GREY assisting the injured girl would not consider the touching to be sexual, making C incorrect, and B is incorrect because if he knew a girl was watching him masturbate it would be an offence under s. 12 of the Sexual Offences Act 2003.

Investigators' Manual, paras 4.2.1 and 4.4.2

57. Answer **A** — It is an offence at common law falsely to imprison another person. False imprisonment can be committed intentionally or recklessly. A lawful arrest will provide a defence to the *offence* as will reasonable defence of property. In respect of the latter, a person would have a defence to a charge of false imprisonment if he/she detained a person in a genuine belief that a person was a burglar—even if this genuine belief was unreasonable (*R v Shwan Faraj* [2007] EWCA Crim 1033). Making A the correct answer.

Investigators' Manual, para. 3.4

58. Answer **B** — The Serious Crime Act 2007, s. 44 states:

(1) A person commits an offence if—
   (a) he does an act capable of encouraging or assisting in the commission of an offence; and
   (b) he intends to encourage or assist its commission.
(2) But he is not taken to have intended to encourage or assist the commission of an offence merely because such encouragement or assistance was a foreseeable consequence of this act.

From this, A appears to be correct; however, s. 51 limits the liability of the offence by setting out in statute the common law exemption established in the case *R v Tyrrell* [1894] 1 QB 710. A person cannot be guilty of an offence in ss. 44, 45, and 46 (Serious Crime Act 2007) if, in relation to an offence that is a 'protective' offence, the person who does the act capable of encouraging or assisting that offence falls within the category of persons that offence (i.e. s.

25 of the Sexual Offences Act 2003, see para. 4.5.5) was designed to protect and would be considered the victim. A is therefore incorrect. C is incorrect as the offence is made out when intentionally encouraged, so cannot be attempted. D is incorrect as stepbrother and stepsister consensual sex cannot be permitted until the 'victim' is 18 years old, making B the correct answer.

Investigators' Manual, para. 1.3.2

59. Answer **D** — The only defence to the taking of an image, etc. of a person under 18 years of age in both s. 1 of the Protection of Children Act 1978 or s. 160 of the Criminal Justice Act 1988, is that they are married or living in an enduring relationship. Therefore B and C are incorrect. With regard to undeveloped film, for s. 1 of the Protection of Children Act you have to be able to prove distribution so the offence would be committed under s. 160 of the Criminal Justice Act 1988: *R v Fellows* (1997). Therefore A would also be incorrect.

Investigators' Manual, para. 4.5.8

60. Answer **A** — Code E para 4.18 states:

Sign the label and ask the suspect and any third party present to sign it also. If the suspect or third party refuses to sign it, an Inspector, or if not available a custody officer, shall be called into the interview room and asked to sign it.

You need to work hard on PACE for the exam; Codes C, D, and E are very popular areas tested and this is an example as to how exact the answer has to be.

Investigators' Manual, para. 1.7.17

61. Answer **C** — Sections 64 and 65 of the Sexual Offences Act 2003 which cover the act of the brother knowingly having sex with his sister and her knowingly allowing him to have sex, carry a maximum of two years in prison. Please note that the answer to this question is hidden in the text and easily missed or forgotten during your revision. There will be between 11 and 15 questions on sexual offences in the exam and, unlike other subjects, it is not as vast as other areas of law for your syllabus, so needs intricate revision tactics.

Investigators' Manual, para. 4.5.6

62. Answer **A** — The Theft Act 1968, s. 5(3) states:

Where a person receives property from or on account of another, and is under an obligation to the other to retain and deal with that property or its proceeds in a particular way, the property or proceeds shall be regarded (as against him) as belonging to the other.

This is a legal obligation not a moral one and is generally for persons taking deposits and not using them correctly, for example, solicitors, travel agents, etc. However, because the Mall proprietors have stated that the monies will go to a particular cause they have not dealt with the monies in a particular way as intended. Therefore B, C, and D are incorrect. A is therefore the correct answer.

Investigators' Manual, para. 2.1.8

63. Answer **D** — Robbery—s. 8 of the Theft Act 1968 states:

A person is guilty of robbery if he steals and immediately before or at the time of doing so, and in order to do so, he uses force on any person or puts or seeks to put any person in fear of being there and then subjected to force.

Blackmail—s. 21 of the Theft Act 1968 states:

A person is guilty of blackmail if, with a view to gain for himself or another or with intent to cause loss to another, he makes an unwarranted demand with menaces.

A is the offence of blackmail as JONES cannot fear for STAINES; in B and C the offence of robbery is attempted as STAINES is in fear for herself. It is only at D do you have the theft making the full offence of robbery.

Investigators' Manual, paras 2.4 and 2.5

64. Answer **A** — Section 3A of the Bail Act 1976 lists many restrictions a custody officer can impose on a person he is granting bail, and B, C and D are contained in that list. To reside at a bail hostel can only be a condition of bail set by a court. The practical reason for this is that a custody officer does not have the time or the mechanisms for this condition to be put in place.

Investigators' Manual, para. 1.9.7.2

65. Answer **D** — The Sexual Offences Act 2003, s. 25 states:

A person (A) commits an offence if—

- A intentionally touches another person (B);
- the touching is sexual;
- the relation of A to B is within s. 27;
- A knows or could reasonably be expected to know that his relation to B is of a description falling within that section; and
- either—
  - B is under 18 and A does not reasonably believe that B is 18 or over; or
  - B is under 13.

Family members over and above blood relatives include where the defendant and the victim live or have lived in the same household, or the defendant is or has been regularly involved in caring for, training, supervising, or being in sole charge of the victim, and

- one of them is or has been a step-parent;
- they are cousins;
- one of them is or has been the other's stepbrother or stepsister; or
- they have the same parent or foster parent.

Therefore A and C are incorrect as GAIL is only 16. B is incorrect as the Act covers more than blood relatives. D is correct, because for DEVLIN as her stepfather to have lawful consensual sex with GAIL, she would need to have reached the age of 18.

Investigators' Manual, para. 4.5.6

66. Answer **D** — *R v Johnson* [1988] 1 WLR 1377 gave this guidance as to the minimum evidential requirements needed if disclosure is to be protected. This is in order that the police are better

equipped in court not to have to disclose the observation points which could be an issue for the trial.

Investigators' Manual, para. 1.10.8.5

67. Answer **B** — In January 2009 the offence of possession of extreme pornographic images came into force. The offence is set out under ss. 63–67 of the Criminal Justice and Immigration Act 2008. There are three elements as to what an extreme pornographic image is and for it to apply it must fall foul of these:

- the image is pornographic;
- the image is grossly offensive, disgusting, or otherwise of an obscene character; and

the image portrays in an explicit and realistic way, one of the following extreme acts:

— an act which threatens a person's life;
— an act which results in or is likely to result in serious injury to a person's anus, breast, or genitals;
— an act of sexual intercourse with a human corpse (necrophilia; the human must be 'dead');
— a person performing an act of intercourse or oral sex with an animal (whether dead or alive; bestiality).

An image means either a still image or moving images.
Therefore A, C, and D are incorrect. This legislation is relatively new to the National Investigators' Examination so it is worthy of some revision time as it allows new scope for question writers.

Investigators' Manual, para. 4.5.11

68. Answer **C** — The Sexual Offences Act 2003, s. 5 is concerned with rape of a child under 13. Consent cannot be given and there is no defence as to believing the person to be over 13. This makes A and D incorrect. Section 5 covers the same as s. 1, so includes oral sex, making B incorrect.

Investigators' Manual, para. 4.3

69. Answer **D** — The Malicious Communications Act 1988, s. 1 states:

(1) Any person who sends to another person—
    (a) a letter, electronic communication or article of any description which conveys—
        (i) a message which is indecent or grossly offensive;
        (ii) a threat; or
        (iii) information that is false and known or believed to be false by the sender; or
    (b) any article or electronic communication which is, in whole or part, of an indecent or grossly offensive nature.

'Any article' includes dog faeces. Cybercrime is new to the Investigators Manual for 2013 so it is worth in your revision taking time to look at these offences. Note also the defences to the above in paragraph 3.11.4.1. They are very similar to blackmail defences so easily remembered.

Investigators' Manual, para. 3.11.4

70. Answer **A** — The Sexual Offences Act 2003, s. 62 states:

(1) A person commits an offence under this section if he commits any criminal offence with the intention of committing a relevant sexual offence.

(These include aid and abet, counsel or procure.)
Any criminal offence applies, including dangerous driving making B incorrect. Section 62 is a criminal offence with intent to commit a sexual offence so the sexual offence does not have to take place making C incorrect. The fact that there was no kidnap or that LAMBERT is of the age of consent for sex is irrelevant to this question making D incorrect.

Investigators' Manual, para. 4.7.1

71. Answer **B** — The Theft Act 1968, s. 10 states:

(1) A person is guilty of aggravated burglary if he commits any burglary and at the time has with him firearm or imitation firearm, any weapon of offence, or any explosive.

SHADRACK does not commit aggravated burglary when he enters the store room to steal as he does not know he has the weapon of offence with him, making A incorrect. Owing to the concept of 'instant arming', when he steals the handcuffs (made to incapacitate a person per se) he first commits aggravated burglary. At the time of stealing he has a weapon of offence, the fact that the item he is stealing is a weapon of offence, means he commits aggravated burglary at that time. C and D are incorrect as they are not the first point at which aggravated burglary is committed.

Investigators' Manual, para. 2.3

72. Answer **C** — The Serious Organised Crime Act 2005 inserts a new s. 61A into PACE. The section allows the police to take an impression of a person's footwear with or without consent. This applies to any person aged 10 years or over, in police detention, who has either been arrested for, charged with, or informed that he will be reported for a *recordable* offence. Any constable can exercise this power. Therefore A, B, and D are incorrect.

Investigators' Manual, para. 1.8.5

73. Answer **A** — The Fraud Act 2006, s. 11 states:

(1) A person is guilty of an offence under this section if he obtains services for himself or another—
    (a) by a dishonest act, and
    (b) in breach of subsection (2).
(2) A person obtains services in breach of this subsection if—
    (a) they are made available on the basis that payment has been, is being or will be made for or in respect of them,
    (b) he obtains them without any payment having been made for or in respect of them or without payment having been made in full, and
    (c) when he obtains them, he knows—
        (i) that they are being made available on the basis described in paragraph (a), or
        (ii) that they might be,
but intends that payment will not be made, or will not be made in full.

Clearly, to commit an offence contrary to s. 11 of the Fraud Act 2006 it must be a service that is paid for, making A the only correct answer. Remember under the Fraud Act it cannot be attempted as the offence is complete when the false representation is made. Nearly all offences under the Fraud Act are about '*conduct crime*' but for the exception of the services offence where it is about '*result crime*'.

Investigators' Manual, para. 2.6.10

74. Answer **C** — This is aggravated damage under s. 1(2) of the Criminal Damage Act 1971; which deals with the more serious offences of damage with regard to endangering life, either intentionally or recklessly. We tend in the main, because of practical experience, to think of this as arson. The example in the question is a straight lift from the text in the keynote area (*R v Steer* [1988] AC 111).

Investigators' Manual, para. 2.9.3

75. Answer **D** — The Sexual Offences Act 2003, s. 12 states:

(1) A person aged 18 or over (A) commits an offence if—
    (a) for the purpose of obtaining sexual gratification, he intentionally causes another person (B) to watch a third person engaging in an activity, or to look at an image of any person engaging in an activity,
    (b) the activity is sexual, and
    (c) either—
        (i) B is under 16 and A does not reasonably believe B is 16 or over, or
        (ii) B is under 13.

The issue here is whether NELSON committed the offence and if so at what point was it first committed. He knows her to be under 16 and the showing of the images and pictures was for sexual gratification. He can commit the offence by achieving sexual gratification from her watching of the images but, in this question, this was not the case. His motive was to lower the victim's inhibitions. Therefore he commits the offence when he first shows the first image. Image includes a moving or still image and includes an image produced by any means and where the context permits three-dimensional image and it also includes an image of an imaginary person. It does not follow that the sexual gratification has to be immediate, i.e. simultaneous, contemporaneous or synchronised, it can be to put the child in the frame of mind for future sexual abuse (*R v Abdullahi* [2006] EWCA Crim 2060). Making D the correct answer.

Investigators' Manual, para. 4.5.4

76. Answer **B** — The Criminal Justice and Police Act 2001 makes provision for courts to impose travel restrictions on offenders convicted of drug trafficking offences to prohibit the offender from leaving the United Kingdom at any time during the period beginning from his/her release from custody (other than on bail or temporary release for a fixed period) and up to the end of the order.

The minimum period for such an order is two years (s. 33(3)) where a court:

- has convicted a person of a drug trafficking offence; and
- it has determined that a sentence of four years or more is appropriate.

This clearly makes B the correct answer.

In the exam this is the way in which this type of legislation will be tested, rather than problem solving. Ensure that as you learn the Manual that this type of legislation is not missed out, as the examiners can ask any question on anything in the Manual.

Investigators' Manual, para. 3.8.16

77. Answer **C** — The Theft Act 1968, s. 10 states:

A person is guilty of aggravated burglary if he commits any burglary and at the time has with him any firearm or imitation firearm, any weapon of offence, or any explosive.

An air weapon is a firearm for the purposes of s. 10 of the Theft Act 1968 and 'premises' (s. 9 of the Theft Act 1968) includes any building, which is a dwelling, and shall apply also to an inhabited vehicle or vessel and shall apply to any such vehicle or vessel at times when the person having habitation in it is not there as well as at times when he is. There is a general requirement for 'buildings' to have some degree of permanence. An unfurnished house can be a dwelling, as can an industrial freezer (*B and S v Leathley* [1979] Crim LR 314). A and D are incorrect as NICKLIN has committed burglary, and B is incorrect as an air weapon is a weapon of offence for the offence of aggravated burglary.

Investigators' Manual, para. 2.3

78. Answer **A** — When the Public Order Act 1986 was updated following September 11, 2001, creating offences of religious or racial motivation, they missed this one. It refers to a group of persons defined by reference to colour, race, nationality (including citizenship), or ethnic or national origins but **not religion**. This makes B and D incorrect. There does not have to be communication, making C incorrect.

Investigators' Manual, paras 3.7.8 and 3.7.9

79. Answer **C** — Statutory conspiracy — Criminal Law Act 1977, s. 2 (Exemptions from liability for conspiracy).

(1) A person shall not by virtue of section 1 above be guilty of conspiracy to commit any offence if he is an intended victim of that offence.
(2) A person shall not by virtue of section 1 above be guilty of conspiracy to commit any offence or offences if the only other person or persons with whom he agrees are (both initially and at all times during the currency of the agreement) persons of any one or more of the following description.
   (a) his spouse or civil partner;
   (b) a person under the age of criminal responsibility; and
   (c) an intended victim of that offence or each of those offences.

Civil partners and spouses can be convicted of conspiracy if there is a third person, but in this case this includes the intended victim so there is no conspiracy. The fact that the crime does not go ahead is irrelevant once the agreement is made, making A incorrect. If there are separate conspiracies they have to be aware of the common purpose but not each other, therefore B is incorrect, and D is incorrect as the separate conspiracies are persons that cannot be conspired with.

Investigators' Manual, para. 1.3.3.1

80. Answer **B** — The Sexual Offences Act 2003, s. 15 states that a person aged 18 or over (A) commits an offence if, having met or communicated with another person (B) on at least two previous occasions, he intentionally meets B or travels with the intention of meeting B in any part of the world or if B travels with the intention of meeting A in any part of the world. The offence is committed if: at the time, he intends to do anything to or in respect of B, during or after the meeting and in any part of the world, which if done will involve the commission by A of a relevant offence; *B is under 16*; and A does not reasonably believe that B is 16 or over. The communications or meetings can be innocuous, which means there does not have to be any sexual suggestion at that time. A is incorrect as the offence only requires the travelling with the intention; the actual offence does not have to take place. C is incorrect as the content of the communications is irrelevant and the offence includes the victim travelling to the offender. D is incorrect as it is a combination of A and C, making B the correct answer.

Investigators' Manual, para. 4.5.5